Evacuee
Boys

Evacuee Boys

LETTERS OF A FAMILY SEPARATED BY WAR

JOHN E. FORBAT

Front cover photograph: Evacuee boys with their gas masks. (Public information); *back cover photograph*: An Auster like the one John flew. (By kind permission of Mr Phillip Jarrett)

First published 2012

The History Press
The Mill, Brimscombe Port
Stroud, Gloucestershire, GL5 2QG
www.thehistorypress.co.uk

© John E. Forbat, 2012

The right of John E. Forbat to be identified as the Author
of this work has been asserted in accordance with the
Copyrights, Designs and Patents Act 1988.

British Library Cataloguing in Publication Data.
A catalogue record for this book is available from the British Library.

ISBN 978 0 7524 7123 5

Typesetting and origination by The History Press
Printed in Great Britain
Manufacturing managed by Jellyfish Print Solutions Ltd

Contents

Introduction

In August 1939 I had just finished a glorious holiday with friends in Cambridge, for the first time in my life experiencing a real detached house and garden (complete with luscious plum trees). Little did I know, the Second World War was about to be declared.

On 2 September 1939, a day before the Second World War began, my brother and I were evacuated along with thousands of other children from London – our destinations kept absolutely SECRET. Nearly 11 and still a keen Wolf Cub, my evacuation from the anticipated bombing of London, together with my brother Andrew (nearly 15), would be with my school, West Kensington Central School. Reminiscent of the film *Hope and Glory*, mother took us to High Street Kensington station on the District Line, where a milling crowd of evacuees and their parents churned on the platform while authoritative teachers barked orders and tried to keep control. We were each issued with a gas mask in a brown cardboard box – the use of which had been demonstrated amid hilarious farting noises as they breathed out with extra vigour. More interesting was the carrier bag with several large bars of Cadbury's Fruit & Nut chocolate and other goodies to see us through our train journey into the country.

Contrary to the film *Hope and Glory*, mother did not change her mind and, after the District Line took us there, the train pulled out of

Evacuee boys with their gas masks. (Public information)

Ealing Broadway station with the loud steam chuffing of the period, almost drowned by the excited chatter of children embarking upon an adventure. After emigrating from Hungary in 1936, now came another 'emigration'.

We arrived in the small Wiltshire town of Melksham, our worried parents remaining in London. The letters that we sent them, which form this book, graphically depicted our daily lives, the vital importance and difficulties of keeping in touch, and our urgencies and needs – without telephone communication and largely without money for daily necessities. Andrew was the highly conscientious, responsible and thoughtful elder brother who wrote most of the letters, and I was the little tearaway who tried to be good (as far as I was able). Our parents' normal import/ export business was made impossible by the war, so they ran a bridge club in their Kensington rented house and were rather hard up.

Our sporadic letters and postcards still survive. Some are written in Hungarian, some in faded or tattered handwriting; all illustrate our life, trials and tribulations away from our parents and our maternal grandmother, Noni. Often poor spellings and punctuation are reproduced, essentially as we wrote them. Some letters are (childishly) repetitive, others are historically priceless.

Amongst the rest of the contingent from London's West Kensington Central School, we arrived in Melksham by the train from Paddington station. Carrying our suitcases, gas masks and issue of chocolates in bags handed out before the journey, we boys were taken round to various houses where we might be billeted with local families. The government would pay the families 10/- (10 shillings) a week per child. In our case, the first billet only lasted one day, and then we moved into a longer-term billet.

The school had no premises in Melksham, so the location of our schooling was also a problem to be tackled. Most of the younger teachers had been called up for military service, so many of the teachers also moving to Melksham were elderly, some brought out of retirement.

Despite being a fully embedded cockney, with Hungary on the wrong side of the war I soon became classed as an Enemy Alien. The Wiltshire

At the Kellys' with Rosemary. (Author's collection)

burr was also quite foreign and the locals received us *Londonerrrs* with mixed reactions – from 'Do we have to have them here?' to 'Yes, I'll look after these two'. Not unlike the slave trade in reverse, we were taken around house to house where potential foster parents looked us over and, by the end of the day, all of us had somewhere to sleep among families willing to take us in return for 10/- per week. After the first day, Andrew and I were billeted with the family of a (to us) well-to-do factory manager, who aspired to a detached house and their own car, an Austin Ten.

Our letters commenced on 3 September 1939, the day the Second World War was declared.

1

Dear Mum & Dad

Dear Mother and Father,

Fernleigh, 13 Sandridge Road, Melksham Wilts.

First of all, I have to tell you that I changed address as above & I think I shall be much better off in this house. The reason that they put me here is that we only had one single bed for the two of us, & were not very comfortable. I shall come to that later, as I will tell you what I was doing all the time since I got here.

I had quite a pleasant journey, although we were a bit crowded in the tube as you saw at the station. Then at Ealing Broadway, we changed to the GWR [Great Western Railway] which took us right here, without a single stop (except of course at signals).

When we arrived at Melksham, we went to the school buildings & waited there to be put into our billets. While we were waiting, we had tea, milk or water, as we chose. I was called out to talk to a Czechoslovakian girl who has been here for three months. I had to speak to her in German & got on quite well.

The billet I was put into at first was 2 George Street. I had a very nice & kind old lady & she gave me tea as soon as I arrived, that was about three o' clock. We then went for a little walk & came back to put our things into the drawer.

Later in the evening, Mr. Williams & Mrs. Hirst called upon us & asked if we were all right and comfortable. I told him yes & they asked if we had tea, what it was like, what our beds were like & if the landlady was kind.

I told him that we only had one single bed for both of us (which he noted down as a complaint) & that we received tea, which was all right. I told him that I was satisfied otherwise & that the landlady was very kind. We were told to assemble at the Recreation Ground from where we might go the Church. They also asked me if I had any objections to attending a Church of England service. I told them that I was Jewish so I'd rather not. That was arranged too. Mr. Williams seemed to be exceptionally kind yesterday.

We slept quite well in the single bed – not too much & we got on all right. For supper, we had cocoa, bread and butter. I shall write you, what I was doing today, tomorrow, as I want to catch the nine o' clock post.

The address is c/o Mrs. Kelly.

Your loving son
Andrew

… continued by John – his added 'letter' was not quite as informative!
Dear Mum and Dad!

We moved to-day to a better house. Here we have got a lovely big bedroom and a lovely big bed. Mr. Kelly has a car. They have two big gardens, one is full of fruit and vegetables, and the other one has just grass and some trees. There is a little girl of seven years old. Will you write as much as you have time for.

From your loving son,
John

5 September 1939 – a letter from a local gentleman who helped with the billeting of children

I thought you might like to hear from me that both your sons are well, happy and comfortably placed.

They were a little unfortunate in their first billet, but were transferred after the first day or two to a very nice house in one of the best roads in the town.

The people here are wonderfully kind, and cannot do too much for our boys. The lady in charge of the billeting told me that she could have placed almost another thousand of our boys in billets, the people think so highly of them. She was most anxious that every boy should be thoroughly comfortable, and offered to transfer any boy who was not. I have asked the boys over and over again if they are quite happy and comfortable, and they assured me that they were.

This is a quiet little town about 100 miles from London, set amidst some very pleasant scenery.

There is no need for you to feel any anxiety about your sons; they are quite happy and comfortable.

Kind regards and best wishes,
Yours sincerely,
Fred. R. Norton

9 September 1939

Dear Mum & Dad,

I have so far been very disappointed in you for writing so little. I am so anxious to know what is going on at home, & if you don't write, I am worried. I keep on supplying you with fresh news daily & I get no reply at all.

Before I go on writing about myself, I shall urge you to do the following:-

1. Send me a postal order for about half a crown, for I have only got four pence left (& the lucky 3*d* bit which I don't want to spend).[1]
2. Give my best wishes & compliments to Grandfather,[2] Granny[3] & Mariska[4] & tell them, that why I did not write is because I want to confine all my correspondence to English. If they are prepared to have a letter from me in English & have someone to translate it, then let me know by return of post.
3. Send the parcel (containing shirts, bathing costumes & Scout & Cub uniforms) immediately if you have not already done so.
4. Write regularly & keep me informed of what is going on in London.
5. Don't forget to get a gasmask for Grandfather if he has not already got one.
6. I have asked one of my friends (Billy Childs) to call on you occasionally. Receive him kindly & remember that he is one of my best friends & one whom I always wish to keep, for I know that I can count on his help when I need it, just as he can count on mine.
7. I you are in the street during the black-out, be sure that you have a white strip round your arms & waist; it is so much safer.

... *continued on 10 September 1939*

Up to now my usual daily programme was to get up at about eight, assemble with the school at half past nine to receive instructions and announcements, go for a long walk with the school. In the afternoon I have a rest & read. After tea I go to the swings as we call it. The food we get is excellent & plenty.

For three days (Wednesday, Thursday & Friday) I went to a farm to help getting the hay in. I did not like it too much because it was rather far & the fields were very big. Thursday morning the farmer made us (four of us went, John did not, because he is under thirteen) scrub the stables with long brooms. The most unpleasant part is in that was the smell, & the stuff we had to scrub off. However I am not going any more. We only worked three hours a time.

Friday last (the last day on the farm) I had a rest at the wheel of a hay carriage & tried to make a backwards somersault. When I got home I found that I had lost all my money. Luckily I remembered this somersault & next day, I went back to the farm & found every penny of the money which fell out of my pocket. Now I have only got 4*d* because I had to get a shaving set at Woolworths in Bath (as there is none in Melksham) & a nail file.) Please send money immediately, because after posting this & another letter to Childs I shall only have a penny to spend left.

I met Mr. Norton this morning & he told me that he was corresponding with you & that he wrote you that I was in a nice place.

That is quite true for you could not imagine a nicer couple (except you). Mr. Kelly gave me a shilling for postage right on the first day & 6*d* to both of us last Friday to buy sweets. I bought a box of chocolates for Mrs. Kelly on my 6*d* for her birthday on Saturday. They both said I should not have done it, but I am sure she was very pleased.

As I wrote before, we went to Bath yesterday. This is a very nice town, famous for its Roman baths & for its buns. We were in the park & had a look at the Botanical garden.

We have a nice garden in the house (front & back) & in the back garden we have two big apple trees, one for eating & the other for cooking apples.

Mr. & Mrs. Kelly have a very nice LITTLE daughter (7 years old) only a bit wilful & spoilt. We are getting on quite well though.

School will start on Monday. Write me as soon as possible & send money. How is the club & business?

With love and compliments to all,
Andrew & John

24 *September 1939*

Dear Mum & Dad,

I don't think this letter can be quite as long as I promised in my last card, as there is hardly any news to write about.

The most important thing is rather unpleasant but I think you will agree. Mrs. Kelly today said, that the money she gets for billeting us is far too little (17/- for two boys) & that she would like you to contribute with a reasonable amount to our keeping say 5/- for EACH boy a week. She said she hated to do this & she would not have done it were it a question of a few weeks only, but the war might last for years & prices for food are getting higher & higher every day. She said that the other people have said the same – to ask for help from the childrens' parents.

I told her that I understand her position that I shall write home & see what can be done about it, but that I shall NOT promise any regular payments (knowing Daddy's financial position), sometimes the money may be in delay. She said that she would not expect it very regularly, but it would be a great help to her as she has to add a considerable amount to the 17/- from the Government & that she has a lot of extra work in the way of washing, ironing, mending etc.

I think you will understand this & try to send down 10/- a week as often as you can to ease the Kellys' task. You must remember that you have not got to spend money on our food now. Please reply immediately to this as the matter is important.

While we are on the subject of money, my money is gradually going away & probably in a few days' time I shall write for some more money on my last penny. (I shall change the last 2/- now for this letter). I am afraid I could not have my shoes mended this time. It should cost me 3/6 to sole, 1/3 to heel & 4/6 to sole and heel. They said it would be about 4/- for John to have his shoes soled & heeled.

This afternoon we went blackberry picking in the car we came to a hedge which was absolutely full of them. We filled a whole basket from the two sides of the hedge. They were nice big & black ones too.

I fasted from Friday night about 8.30 to Saturday afternoon about 5.30 – just about 21 hours. It was quite easy.[5] I was only hungry at mealtimes. Of course I did not have clear soup & chicken as at home but it was all very nice.

Please do send the bicycle quickly because it would be so nice to have nice long rides in the country. Some boys have already got theirs down.

I told you that I joined the Scouts here, now they elevated me to Patrol Second (next to a Patrol Leader) but this is only for a month to see if I possess natural leadership & I have not got much chance have I? But – at least for a month – I have chance of becoming Patrol Leader as mine said that he did not want to stay in the Troop, so that I might have to take his place. But these are only hopes. By the way, John is a Scout now & not a Cub. He will pass his Tenderfoot soon, when he will be eleven. He is in my patrol too! I am afraid I shall have to do my Journey again as I have not finished my report & so I could not pass it in London & I must do it here. I shall have to re-pass everything I have done in the First Class.

Another thing I must have is my case. I should like you to send me my school case with everything in it but make sure that the blue shorthand book is inside. If it is not, look in my drawers & in the wardrobe but be sure it is there.

I do not think there is anything else to say so I shall close the letter. Excuse John not writing but he is late & I have to be at home at 9.30 & it is 9.20 now so that I shall have to go to the post office in the meanwhile. Give compliments to all, I shall write Noni next time as I am in a hurry & million kisses to you from

Andrew & John

9 October 1939 – at last a card from John

Dear Mum and Dad,

I am only writing a post-card because there isn't any news besides that the bicycle has not arrived yet. In the last few days it has been raining a terrible lot. My finger is much better and there is nothing to worry about. I miss you very much, please come as soon as you can. How is business? How is Granny, Grand Dad and Mariska?

I got a letter from Mr. Young yesterday and answered it to-day.[6] I left room for Andrew on the other side.

Yours dearly loving son,
John

… continued by Andrew

Dear Mum & Dad,

I have asked John to write the main part of the card today. It will do him good. There is no other news besides what John writes.

Thousands of kisses from,
Andrew

23 October 1939

Dear Mother & Father,

Mrs. Childs probably told you already that I had a quarrel with
Mr. Kelly, but I want to tell you that since then, things have been much
quieter again. As to what I can make of it, Mr. Kelly has many moods.
Sometimes he is in a good mood & sometimes he is in a bad one. He
was very angry about me taking Mrs. Childs up into the unfinished
room & he used this occasion to say everything that he wanted to say.
He did not shout or use nasty words. He said it all in a quiet polite tone.
He accused me of not being straight forward because I did not tell either
him or Mrs. Kelly about your coming, about Bill coming, & instead of
asking first I just brought Bill & his mother in. All they knew about the
arrival of Mrs. Childs was what they could pick up from conversation
between John & me. Secondly, he accused me of taking everything for
granted & that I have no consideration for Mrs. Kelly. As an instance
he put forward that I did yesterday morning. He also said that I did not
offer any help to her & took all I could.

He had no grudge against Johnny, because he was too young to know
these things, but he thought I was old enough. He kept on sermonising
for about an hour mentioning that he definitely objected to me talking
about him as landlord & Mrs. Kelly as landlady. He said he was no
landlord to us until we paid anything like £2 a week. As we are now, we
are only in his house through his charity & kind-heartedness.

As a final point he mentioned something I did not understand saying:
'When you came here I did not take you as Jews, but as children in
distress. If your conduct has been such as to alter this attitude, it was
your own fault.' What do you make of that?

After dinner I saw Mrs. Childs again and told her the whole story
asking her to give you a note & to tell you all about it. It is a pity you
were not here yesterday. I was very sorry that you could not come, but it
was comforting to see some of my old friends.

At tea-time, Mr. Kelly seemed to have forgotten all about the quarrel
but I did not. I pretended to be very distressed, & only had one cup of

tea & took no cake. Of course he noticed it & when he got up he said, 'What I told you at dinner does not concern you now' & he stroked my head. After tea I have done the drying for Mrs. Kelly & everything was OK. We have not talked about the quarrel since.

Before I forget, will you please send that card which I gave you before I left London, to be completed when National Registration takes place, to the Schoolkeeper in London [to W.K. Central School].

Thank you very much for the things you sent down. The cake is excellent. I am afraid Daddy's pullover would do as a skirt for me. It is so big.

Will you please send the money down for this week soon, as a week has elapsed since the last 10/- to Mrs. Kelly. I shall not have much left when I bought another lot of stamps for postcards. By the way – Mrs. Childs gave us 1/- to share and I put in savings. If you think I should not have accepted it, give it back to her.

Make sure you have your seats booked at Mrs. Shaw for next month, as I want to see you soon. What about me coming down for the half term holiday? I could spend two whole days with you.

Mrs. Kelly said that if we were to go down for Christmas week & stay at home for a week, she would give us the weekly Government allowance of 17/- for fares. I thanked her very much though I said that I did not think Daddy would take it.

For a long time you have not told me how the club was going. I am interested in that. Do not think John can sign this letter & I want to send it now, as I do not want to read it to John in case someone in the house overhears it.

I do not want to be moved from Mrs. Kelly for I do not think I can get a better home than this one, although I should not like to have another quarrel like this one. I tried to defend myself but he interrogated me whenever I started to speak.

Write me soon & lots of love & kisses,
from Andrew

26 October 1939 – a postcard

Dear Mum and Dad,

I am very sorry I am so late in writing but I was awaiting your reply to my letter and the something you going to send. I hope the something stands for money.

I hope when I get the letter, it will say that I can come down for the weekend, for this is a chance not likely to recur before Xmas and I am very eager to see you.

If I get your 'yes' before to-morrow morning's school, I shall come straight away. If I get it after school I shall come on Saturday. If I get a 'no' than I shall be ever so disappointed.

There is no other news. Mr. & Mrs. Kelly are still very kind. I wish I could see you this weekend.

Lots of love from Andrew

… continued by John on the back of the postcard

Dear Mum & Dad,

I miss you terribly come as soon as possible. I feel very well, how are you? It has been rather cold the last few days what is it like in London? Is everybody alright? Please send money as we are very hard up. If you have already sent it take it as unwritten.

John

28 October 1939

Dear Mum and Dad,

Thank you very much for your letter and the money we received this morning. I am afraid I was rather disappointed that I could not see you this weekend. It was a very good chance that I missed. As a matter of fact, at first I wanted to come, thinking that you wanted me to come only you dare not say no. I feel just the same about visiting you, as you describe in your letter to me. All last night, the night before and before that I was thinking of home, how nice it would be to be home – even thought for a short while – and how I should like to see you again. I was seeing it all in front of me, and I nearly thought myself to be at home as I saw you all before my eyes. I did not forget anybody. I even saw little Tiggy under the bed cover meowing when I touched her.[7] I saw you two, Granny, Mariska, Bene,[8] the whole house, a good Hungarian meal & I felt myself at home I hope I can come for Christmas with Johnny and spend a happy week together.

This afternoon I went [to] Trowbridge and saw at the pictures, 'The Four Feathers'. It is an excellent picture. At the same time, I went to Woolworths, bought a lock for the bike (6d) at Curry's a bicycle pump (1/3) and battery (3d) for reserve in case I cannot get one later when the first one is exhausted and paid 6d to go to pictures. I also bought a Scout hat for 3/- and gave John 2/- for saving up for his watch, which he wants to buy when has enough money. (I thus have 2/6d left but do not be frightened for that will last me until you send some more.)

While I was in Trowbridge, John borrowed Mr. Kelly's bike and went to Bath with some other Scouts and went to the Roman bath where he had a little swimming. He learned to dive, to swim on his back, to float on his back and to swim under water. He seems to have had a jolly good time. Usually on Saturdays Mr. Kelly lends John his bike so that we can go for a ride together. We have already been to Calne, Chippenham, Trowbridge, Bradford-on-Avon and Bath. I shall have to go to Devizes, Westbury and Warminster before I shall finish off all the nearby towns.

I am now listening to 'Bandwagon'. It is excellent. Do you ever listen to that?

I was writing to you before about the club we have formed at school. It is on Mondays and Wednesdays for seniors from 6.30 to 8 p.m. For Juniors it is on Tuesdays and Thursdays from 6 to 7 p.m. There we play cards, draughts, chess. We can read, or write letters. It is supposed to be an evening activity so that we should not be too bored in the long winter nights. We have also got a library in school and I took out some 'Tales of Tolstoy'.

When you come next month I hope you will come on Sunday 26th November. I think you can arrange with Mrs. Shaw (I understand she hires the bus for November) that the bus should come on Johnny's birthday.

The violin will come useful now as we shall try to organise the school orchestra. As I am the only one here who can play the violin decently, I shall probably be asked TO GIVE LESSONS to the others. Band practices will be carried on, on Monday nights from 6–7.

I have been on very good terms with Messrs Kelly since that last quarrel. It seems to me that to some extent it was due to bad mood on his part and besides he did not feel very well that day. However since then we have nearly forgotten. I do not understand quite what you mean by taking them more into my confidence. They already know that Daddy and Mummy have to work all night because of the club and that we have to keep the club because business is absolutely 'pong'. I told them that the club means that we have to keep a big house, the big house that we have to pay big rent, big rates & taxes and have to keep a maid, so that we are hard up, but of course I did not say that we are full of worries with regard to creditors like Mr. Creswell, or that we have not paid the rent for so many months, that Mariska has not hade to have her wages for so many weeks, that the telephone is often shut down etc.

This reminds me – is the telephone all right now?

... continued in Hungarian

I think that it would be good to write a little in Hungarian, otherwise I shall forget a lot. I think that we are rarely alone, so that we are speaking Hungarian then. I don't mind that and I am glad if you write to me in Hungarian.

I would very much like to see you all and to speak with you. I have thought of telephoning you but I hear that it costs 4/6*d* to telephone and there is no telephone in our house, so you can't telephone me either. Today I am writing a few more letters to those in the house. So I won't write any more to you today.

A million kisses from Andrew

29 *October 1939*

Dear Mum and Dad,

Thank you very much for the money you sent us. Yesterday Andrew cycled down to Trowbridge and saw the 'Four Feathers'. At the same time, I cycled down to Bath with some Scouts on Mr. Kelly's bicycle. At Bath we parked the cycles and walked down to the swimming bath. We went in for sixpence. I[t] was a very nice pool, and the water was lovely and warm. I had quite a lot of fun. I was in for about a half a hour. In this time I learned (taught myself) how to dive head first, swim on my back, to swim under the water with my eyes open, and to swim on my side. I think that this was worth sixpence. When we came out we went to see the Roman Baths for sixpence it was very interesting. I saw the healing water. I[t] was steaming hot and it had to be cooled before using. I am knitting a doll's jumper.

Your dearly loving son,
John

29 October 1939 – written in Hungarian

Dear Mummy & Daddy,

I thought I would write a few lines today, before I close off this thick letter, though nothing particular has happened.

The weather was so bad today, that we did not go anywhere by bike, I knitted and read all day. I shall only go out in the evening, to post the letters, as I have written to Mariska that as usual, the menu was very good on Sunday. In general we get good meals, but of course, the English food cannot be as nice as the Hungarian.

I hope you do not worry in this is late. Don't worry in any case if you don't get news for a few days, if sometimes I only write every other day and the post is not very punctual.

Many kisses,
Andrew

5 November 1939 – written in Hungarian

Dear Mummy and Daddy,

I hope you are not too cross that I have not written for so long since Daddy's visit and I hope that you did not worry. I told Daddy that there is no need to worry if there is no post for a day or two, particularly if a Sunday falls in between.

I was very pleased with Daddy's visit but it is a pity it was so short. I am also very pleased that Mummy will come down in the week and I think that Thursday would be the most convenient day.

The Beigli is so good, that hardly any of it remains.[9] Naturally we offered it to the Kellys too and they liked it very much. Next time Mummy, bring some Női Szeszély[10] cake and another loaf of Beigli, so that it should last a little longer.

Yesterday we went to the cinema in Trowbridge. We saw Charles Laughton in 'Jamaica Inn'. A very good film. Next week we shall also see a good film and I see that the following few weeks, lots of such films are coming, which ran for weeks in London.

Yesterday, I allowed myself a small luxury as besides the cinema, I bought chocolate for 2*d* in Trowbridge and 3*d* worth of chips and with Johnny and Rosemary, we ate them.

We got up late today and it was nearly 11 o'clock before we finished breakfast. It was nice weather and I went out cycling. I went from Melksham to Devizes and from there back via Chippenham. It was about 25 miles and took about 2½ hours. On the way, I bought some chocolate for 3*d* as I was hungry and to put new life into me. So now 10*d* remains. Isn't it terrible that money goes so fast? Yet tomorrow, I have to buy a ticket.

I was unable to cash the cheque at Barclays in Trowbridge. They said that one can only get cash at a Covent Garden Branch, so Mr. Kelly will put it into his own account probably tomorrow, so there should still be 10/- in the bank, in case he deposits it later. I would not like such a mistake next time, with the cheque coming back again. It will be best if Mummy will bring cash, because a cheque always caused difficulties.

I have no more to write today, so many kisses till we see you.

Andrew

… continued by John

Excuse me writing in English, but it is much easier. When Mummy comes on Friday please bring some 'Feminine Spirit' cake. Today Andrew went to Divizes [sic] on the bicycle and from Devizes to Chippenham and back to Melksham. It was all together about twenty-five miles. Yesterday Andrew and I cycled down to Trowbridge Andrew on our bicycle and I on Mr. Kelly's. It only took us about half an hour to get there. When we got to Trowbridge we wend to the 'New Kinema' and saw the picture called 'Jamaica Inn'. I[t] was a very good and exiting film. Andrew has finished the cardigan, and he has started on the front of the pullover. The pullover that mummy knitted for Granddaddy does not fit me but it fits Andrew quite well it is beautifully knitted. I am writing a little letter to Raymond[11] will you please give it to Mr. or Mrs. Newnham and ask them to send it to Raymond.

Yours dearly loving son,
John

16 November 1939 – written in Hungarian

Dear Mummy and Daddy,

Firstly there has been no important change in the position. I got your letter today and was very pleased that you will be visiting us on Sunday after all. I think that I made a little mistake in my letter, that Mrs. Kelly cannot receive you. I should have written that she cannot receive you on Sunday, since she works a lot all week; she gets up a little later on Sunday and the house is not ready till much later. So she would have much more work, if she gave you lunch, she would not get her Sunday rest. That is why she does not want it to be Sunday when you come.

I therefore told her that I don't want her to make lunch for you especially, just that you should be able to go up to my room and that we could talk. To this she said, if you come, you come and she cannot do anything against it.

I asked her whether she has spoken with the billeting officer and she said that she spoke and they told her that she must make application in writing and this must be done quickly. I don't care any more, since I am tired of the whole family, especially the little girl; the most hateful, and besides, badly behaved. She does not obey anybody and she does what she wants.

Bring more pastries, some 'feminine spirit' cake and a small Beigli. [12] I think that we could come to London for the weekend of Johnny's birthday. But where shall we sleep if the McDougalls and the Figgins are living there?

What is Tiggy doing? Are the kittens there yet? Write before you come.

Today I think that we will take all of our things up to our room and pack everything that is not in everyday use, so that we may be able to move at any moment.

Many, many kisses till we see each other,
Andrew

… continued by John – also written in Hungarian

Dear Mum and Dad,

I cannot write much today because Andrew wrote about everything. I am very pleased that you are coming down on Sunday and I think that we can come down for my birthday and stay for the weekend. But I don't know where we will sleep if McDougals and Figgins are there.

Many kisses from your loving John

Overnight Travels to London by Lorry, 2/-

Andrew and I got to hear of a cheap way to get to London, using a local trucking company, Crooks, that made overnight journeys to London and then similar journeys back. We made more than one such visit home, riding in the cab with the lorry driver. While mother in London never ceased to worry, the driver was always very nice and very proper throughout these journeys, even stopping at dawn so that we could see the sunrise. Eventually we would arrive in Kensington, where mother would be waiting anxiously in the street. In those days nobody thought about, let alone experienced, any problems with paedophiles or other reasons to doubt the integrity of such a route.

6 December 1939 – written in Hungarian

Dear Mummy,

I am writing to you separately on the occasion of your birthday tomorrow. I wish you a long and happy life, health – and money. If this happens, then surely we will all be happy together.

We shall arrive late for your birthday, so I'll say my little verse personally, which I say every year. (I am small still).

We shall probably arrive at a similar time as before, but maybe later. I shall not send a telegram, so don't be worried. I cannot write you the exact time of my arrival. It could be a lot later, because I don't know for sure when we shall be starting out.

A boy told me today that he spoke with Mr. Redfearn,[13] who told him that we shall have two weeks Christmas holidays. I think this would be wonderful. We will discuss everything at home. I gave the money to Mrs. Kelly today, but we must take the value of the stamp out of savings. (We borrowed 1½d for the stamp from Mrs. Kelly instead of taking it out of savings). So I won't write any more this week. It won't be worth while.

Once again, I wish you the most beautiful future and send you man[y] kisses,
Andrew

… *continued by John*

Dear Mum and Dad,

I wish you Mummie many happy returns, and the best of luck, and I wish you to live very long in happiness and health. Why didn't you send us any money: We are penniless. And we shall have to take some money out of the savings to post this letter.

We shall see you on Friday. And Mr. Crook said that we could come every fortnight. Andrew tells me that a friend said that a master said that we might have a fortnights holiday for Christmas.

Many kisses from your loving son,
John

The Birds and the Bees

Quite a prudish lady, Mrs Kelly called hiccups 'hic coughs', to be ever so 'correct'. For me, this blissful environment only lasted a few weeks until with insatiable curiosity for the unknown: I disgraced myself by peeping into the bathroom while their 7-year-old daughter was being bathed. Mrs Kelly saw this and *was not amused*. Shortly afterwards, I was kicked out and relegated to Widow Trimnell in her seventeenth-century cottage without heating, one cold tap in the outhouse and an outside toilet down the garden.

The bitter 1939/40 winter blew past the blackout blinds through the cracks around the doors and frosted up windows. To maintain a semblance of warmth, I went to my shared bed with another evacuee, fully dressed under my pyjamas. The lodger in the other bed added some warmth to the little room and the chamber pot steamed visibly after every use. The partition wall to Mrs Trimnell's bedroom nearly broke through whenever Harold, my bed companion, and I rolled into it as we fought and wrestled – leading to much Wiltshire yelling coming back through the wall.

Morning wash was a one-finger affair in the freezing outhouse, while the holes in my socks – worn through during the wintry 'nice long walks' on which I was sent – were hardly noticeable by virtue of the accumulated dirt on my heels. Andrew rectified this on occasion, dragging me to the public baths and scrubbing me off with carbolic soap.

18 December 1939

Dear Mum & Dad,

To-day's news may be a bit of a surprise and a shock for you, but take it calmly as it is not as bad as it sounds. The billeting officer has suddenly found a place for John, and he was moved last Saturday. The reason for my silence up to now was that I wanted to find something out about the new billet.

Before I go any further, however I should like to point out that the <u>sudden</u> removal was just as much a surprise to Mrs. Kelly as it was to me or John.

I am afraid that the place is by no means suitable for a long stay. It is a fairly small house, which is as old as its owner (actually the house must be a few hundred years old, and the landlady nearly as old). There is another boy living with John, who is quite a decent chap. But coming back to the house itself – John has a nice big bed, which he shares with his friend. There is no bathroom (there are very few houses in Melksham that have) and it has a nice and warm sitting-dining room. He was cold in his bed for the first two nights, so I gave him my brown blanket & told him to put his dressing-gown and his two coats over him & if he is still cold, that he should ask the woman to get him some Army blankets from the Town Hall, which are issued free. Of course you cannot expect to be warm this weather.

He gets decent plain food and plenty of it. The people seem to be very poor – the whole place is a poor dump – so that he cannot get any dainties or luxuries, but he gets quite good cheap food. The chief complaint from both boys seems to be that.

Turning to other subjects after such an enthusiastic page, I must inform you that our cash now amounts to 2*d* which will just suffice for a 1½*d* stamp on my next letter in which I shall say when we are coming.

It will be either Thursday night or Friday night. I shall have to see Mr. Crook first. However, I should be grateful, if you would enclose in your next letter, which I hope you will write as soon as you get this one, a Postal Order, in which you let Mrs. Kelly have some money as well as me. I have not asked her whether she wants 10/- or only 5/- a week in future, however short the future may be.

Now I shall go over to John to put some of his writing in here too.

Until my next letter, countless kisses from
Andrew

P.S. Do NOT worry about John. He will be all right.

19 December 1939

Dear Mum & Dad,

I went to Mr. Crook[14] & asked him of I could go on Thursday night, & he said that he cannot undertake to take me at night, as there have been a number of accidents lately, & he would be worried to death if I were to go. He advised me to go by rail, & then I shall be safe. I have no time to write all that must be said now, but I can assure you that it is not his fault.

I went down to the Rly. Station & asked how much it will be for both of us to go down & it will be 16/10*d* return for both. So PLEASE send £1 as soon as you get the letter so that I may travel on Friday morning. I shall just get it in time, if you post it <u>as soon as</u> you receive this letter.

Thanking you in advance,
Andrew

P.S. We shall arrive Friday morning. I do not know when yet. Thanks for your card this morning.

6 January 1940

(Dear Ma, I'm having lots of fun I'm sending you the Siegfried Line[15] to hang your washing on.)

Dear Mum & Dad,

Thank you very much for your letter of yesterday morning. I should like you to send me some money if I cannot present the cheque, as after having posted this letter our total fortune will be $1\frac{1}{2}d$, just enough to write another letter.

I have seen Mr. Clark[16] again & he said that he will do his best to move John from that place as soon as possible.

We were having quite a good lot of entertainment this week, including film shows, lectures, 1 party & dancing. John has been to pictures twice this week & I once – I should appreciate, that if you send money, you would state how much belongs to me and how much to John. This pleasure is not going to last much longer, as next week school proper starts again & I shall have to study hard for the Cambridge [School Certificate].

I can hardly think of any other news, so – lots of love from

Andrew

14 January 1940

Dear Mum & Dad,

Thank you very much for the money received on Saturday. I received our telegram too, which you must have sent shortly before my letter arrived, as I posted one Friday morning. I am sorry I caused you worry really there was no need for it.

Rosemary had a party yesterday, we had some nice things to eat. John was there too however I had to leave after tea, as I had to go to a Scouts party, where we had a lot of games. I had a nice present too from Mr. Kelly – everyone got something – an aeroplane constructing set. John had one too.

We are getting quite a lot of homework now, & I am sure we shall have more later on.

John has not been moved yet. I shall have to see the billeting officer again to-morrow.

I cannot think of anything else to write (oh yes! I sent you the bill for my watch instead of John's guarantee. Please send me one back. Also please send my shaving brush, and 2 collars I left at home. Hope I can cash the cheque soon, as I want socks, handkerchiefs, Scout trousers, watch repairs money, & other things too that I cannot think of just now). John has been to pictures twice this week & I have not been at all. His landlady wants him out of doors most of the time. That's why he gets the money to go to pictures. (He always has to go for nice long walks.)

I don't think there is anything else so lots of love & kisses & don't be angry – from Andrew.

... *continued in German*

Dear Noni,

Thank you for your letter. I have not had such a good time on New Year's Eve as you. I was in bed. I did not celebrate the New Year at all. One can do nothing about it. Be calm, I think about you when I don't write. I am just too lazy and I have homework to do as well.

Your Andrew

21 January 1940

Dear Mum & Dad,

I hope you received John's letter on Saturday so that you did not worry over the weekend. Thank you for the 2/- as well for which I did not have a chance to thank you yet. I had 9*d* left to see 'The Spy in Black' with John tomorrow. I am sorry to say but money does not seem to last long. I hope I can cash the cheque soon, as I want some socks, handkerchiefs, Scout shorts, a spare pair of trousers, mending wool, bicycle repairs, shirts for Johnny etc. rather badly. Please send a little more next letter.

I have talked enough about money so I shall leave that for a while. I have arranged for John to be able to have a bath at Melksham House every Thursday for 3*d*. Starting next Thursday. That will be his first bath since we came back from London. I do hope he will be moved soon, or alternatively that you will bring him back to London, as he does not seem to be happy in that place. He says that it makes his heart ache when he comes to get some current bread at the bakers. Nevertheless, I beg you not to ask Mrs. Kelly to take John back, as she cannot be expected to do it & she will not do it. – John was here this morning & he got a cup of tea just before he went out. He said, he did not enjoy a cup of tea for a long time like he did this one.

I think it was one of our coldest days this morning & all the pipes froze up. Mr. Kelly had to warm them with the blow lamp, so that we could have a little water.

The first part of John's scholarship was on Thursday, in which he thinks he passed. The second part will only be open to those who passed the first one & will take place in the middle of March.

All masters are back from their holidays now, & I expect to have a lot of homework now onwards. I shall have to work jolly hard if I want to pass. I am sure I don't know what I am going to do if I do pass. Shall I go to a University, & if so, what line shall I take? I have not made up my mind upon this subject yet.

How is Mummy's fountain pen writing? I hope it is all right – apropos, it is Mr. Kelly's birthday next Sunday the 28th when I hope to see you and I hope you will write me in time when the bus arrives.

Mummy please bring us some nice cakes on Sunday, & get some sandwiches for yourself, as I did not ask Mrs. Kelly to get a meal ready for you. Of course, now we know that you can go to the King's Arms, for a cup of tea. Oh boy, I <u>am</u> looking forward to next Sunday, & I guess so are you!

How is all the family getting on? What did Granny say when she heard the explosions? I guess she was scared stiff thinking that they were bombs. How is Grandpa doing? Is he going back to Budapest?

Hoping that nothing intervenes to stop you coming next Sunday.

I remain yours lovingly,
Andrew

P.S. I have no more stamps so please send money. Send my watch ticket back please, as I can't get my watch without.

8 February 1940

Dear Mum & Dad,

I received your card this morning, telling me about your enquiry. I personally think, that you are right in waiting for another week or so, as there is a good possibility of him being moved shortly now, as I think Dr. Cavell (my class master) has found him a billet, & probably I shall soon hear about it. Mr. Redfearn yesterday told me that they do not want John taken back, as really he will get the best education he can get at all in Melksham. I should prefer John to stay, as I feel I shall miss him having no one to take care of, & being here quiet alone, but John, I think wants to go home, rather than get moved. If I were you, I should keep him here, unless it is absolutely necessary to act reversely.

Yesterday, I went in for the Ambulance Badge at Scouts, & successfully passed it. This is a very important & useful badge. I am very glad I've got it.

Thank you very much for your 2/-, it was not enough to buy all the clothes & things I wanted, but still we have only 3d each left, after having bought some soap & toothpaste, stamps & little sweets. My torch is still without a battery, & my shoes want mending badly, & I have to wear my new pair now. John had his shoes mended, but he says they are too small now.

I think John is writing a letter to-night as well. He said he was going to complain that he is fed up, & that he won't stand for it any longer, but I should not take him too seriously. I think he is just annoyed by the fact, that the other boy had a fight with him for apparently no serious reason, & being older than John, he proved stronger. I promised John that he would not stay in that place long now.

I am getting quite a lot of homework each night now, & am getting on well. To-day we had drawing, but as the drawing teacher has retired, we had the girls' mistress. I think she is much better than Mr. Williamson. She does some explaining, while he tells you to get on with it. I was told that my English essays are all right, & the history master said (after marking a history essay of mine) that my English has improved tremendously. I suppose that is because I always speak English now.

In consequence of the homework I get, I cannot do much knitting, but I have reason to believe that the jumper will be finished this week-end, unless I am overworked with homework.

I am very sorry to hear that Grandfather went back to Budapest yesterday. I think that he should have stayed. The weather is not suitable for him to travel now either. I only hope I shall see him again next summer. It is a pity too that business is so bad. Really there should have been some improvement with the time of the year – This reminds me – when can I cash the cheque? I need the money!

What is the weather like in London? It is quite mild here, & today for the first time the pavements were nice & clear. Owing to the thaw that set in, the river & the canal have flooded, but I do not think that any serious damage has been done.

I do not think there is anything else that will interest you, so all the best wishes, & give my love to everybody. Thousands of kisses to you until we meet again.

From Andrew

P.S. I hope you can read my scribble.

15 February 1940 – written in Hungarian

Dear Mummy and Daddy,

Mummy wrote such a nice letter in English that I write in English with astonishment. Just in John's letter were there some errors in expression but the English is very good. Thank you for the money and for the handkerchiefs.

Johnny has not moved from his place yet, but as I wrote earlier, wait since only a few days will pass till the billeting officer will get better. Hopefully everything will be in order by the 20th, but if not, a few days later. Poor Dr. Cavell has got so tired, that it would be poor behaviour if we did not wait for a week or two, and he has been trying to help us.

I would like to know, if the Easter Holiday is long enough, then you think that we could go camping with the 10th Fulham Saturday, Sunday and Monday. I still have no certainly and there may not be a camp, but probably, but Mr. Young already wrote that if possible he will arrange a camp half way between London and Melksham, and then the London and the evacuated children can camp together. In this case, I could be home by Monday afternoon. This is just a proposal, but I would like to know your opinion.

Write to say if I am writing correctly in Hungarian, because I would like to take a Hungarian exam in December, and I want to know, if my language and spelling are good enough and that I don't use English rules translated into Hungarian. Since we are in Melksham, I now speak English so much that often English comes easier than Hungarian.

Exceptionally, yesterday I got a battery for the bicycle lamp which cost 9*d*. John bought himself a Scout diary for a shilling, and I spent one penny on a collar being cleaned (I had 3*d*), so that between us we have 4*d*.

I am pleased that the bridge tournament idea was successful, and I hope that this will repeat many times. Perhaps if somebody knows that he could only lose his friend's money, then he will come. How could Mr. Haes have won the first prize? Perhaps he became a good player, that he won the prize? [The final page of the letter is missing.]

21 February 1940 – written in Hungarian

Dear Mum and Dad,

A thousand apologies, that I have now written for such a long time. I was waiting for John's letter and I did not have much time. Anyway I won't wait for John's letter.

For now, John is still in that place, but it should be possible for him to move this week or next week. Wait a while, till things are in order.

Thanks very much for the 4/6, For now I am not spending much from I, but the reason why I wanted it was that at last, I shall be able to get my watch, which has been in the shop since 1st January. I miss it.

I see from the calendar with pleasure, that only one month remains till the Easter holiday and then with the earliest bus, we shall get together. I must finish now as I have to go to school.

Many, many kisses sent by your Andrew

P.S. The cream slice and the sugar cake are very lovely.

February 1940 – written in Hungarian

Dear Mummy and Daddy,

I received Mummy's letter today and I am very sad, that you think that I did not write because I have cooled away from you and because I am not interested in you. My letters are short, because there is no particular news. Every day we do the same and there is no variation or news. John has not had a bath since he did at Melksham House, because the times are reserved for soldiers. I am going to Mr. Clark again and ask him if it is not possible to for Daddy to talk with him John moving with him, that John might be able to move. Mrs. Trimnell also now wants him to go, because she could get a lodger in place of the two children and that would pay her more. Daddy should also talk about this, but I don't know how much that would help. Next week we begin exams, always in March. I hope to be top boy, but I am not sure of this. John also has exams, but it is not sure that he will come first, because he has only been in the class since Christmas.

I told John to write also, so that we can post a letter today.

Daddy, please bring enough money so that I can get my watch out and John would like you to leave his watch with the watchmaker in London, not where you bought the watches.

Unfortunately I cannot write any more because I have to go to evening school and it is already quarter to six. We have to do a small play for the smaller boys.

I don't have time to write to Noni, I'll write next time and till then I send my respects.

Andrew sends many, many kisses

26 February 1940 – two pairs of tattered letters with pieces missing.
Andrew's in Hungarian, John's in English

Dear Mummy & Daddy,

Actually I did not write, because I was waiting for news from home. Unfortunately, John has still not moved, I hope they will do something on Saturday. They usually move on Saturdays. We are glad that Daddy will come on Sunday. Now that the weather is nicer, I hope there will be no impediment. … there may be an opportunity on Thursday and we shall see what can be done.

We went to the pictures on Saturday, and saw two very good films. We may go today too, if I don't have enough money, then John will go – I don't know.

Speaking of money, I have 2 pence, but Johnny has 1/-. Of course if we go to the cinema, then I shall only have 2d from which 1½d I'll spend on the stamp. There is not much more to write, so I am leaving John some room.

Many, many kisses and don't be cross,
Andrew

Dear Mum and Dad,

I am sorry I haven't written yet. I have not been moved yet. We cleaned the bicycle on Saturday and it isn't so rusty. I am glad that Dad is coming on Sunday.

Lots of love to everybody from,
John

P.S. I am writing so badly because I am writing <u>on a wall</u>.

Undated and pieces missing

We are progressing well at school, I can now prove Pythagoras' Theorem. The difference is just that we call it Pejszagorasz. Besides this, we are progressing well in Algebra and we are solving quite difficult equations. The English teacher said that I may have a chance to pass in English, but the rest …? I 'took' a little of this, because till then, I thought I might pass in English … will try to write – but that will require more stamps and my money will be used up more quickly. And I cannot writ either without buying stamps and envelopes.

I am leaving space for John, for tomorrow too.

Love and kisses,
Andrew

… continued by John

Dear Mum and Dad,

We than[k] you for the money you sent and the handkerchiefs. Yesterday I bought myself a Scouts diary for 1/-.

Unfortunately I have not been moved yet, and if I don't get moved shortly than bring me home. I am fed up with waiting and with Mrs. Trimnell.

Sunday she tries to make me go to Church and when I told her that I was of a different religion, she said she does not care. Yesterday she sent me out for a walk again. Lately she never boils any water for the hot water bottle and if I ask for it, she said that I don't need it.

I therefore have to sleep with shirt and pullovers and the dressing-gown on. Sometimes she doesn't wake us until about half past eight and I am late for school. I have no more room to write, so goodbye till we meet again.

Lots of love and kisses to everyone,
from John

The seventeenth-century cottage after post-war renovation. (Author's collection)

29 February 1940

Dear Mum and Dad,

I am very glad that Dad is coming to Melksham on Sunday. Will you please do your best to bring my watch down, as I miss it a great deal.

I have not been moved yet, and I am glad that if I am not moved by the exam, I shall come home.

How are you all getting on? How are Tiggy and the kittens? I am all right.

To-day it has been snowing but it did not settle Thank you very much for the money. I am glad Grand-dad arrived home safely. How is Mariska? Send her my love.

Lots of love to everybody,
John

P.S Send my best love to Noni.

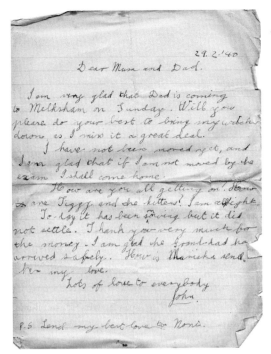

John's original letter of 29 February 1940. (Author's collection)

A modern 1939 council house. (Author's collection)

Soon After

Eventually rewarded for my constant pestering of the billeting officer, I was moved to the luxury of Mrs Robbins' council house before I froze to death.

Beginning of March 1940

Dear Mum & Dad,

At last I am able to write some good news, because it is safe to say that John will be moved this Saturday. His new billet will be in Martigny Road, at Mrs. Robins & although I have not been there yet, and I do not know the people, I am told that they are nice people, & as to the house, it is a fairly new one, & has a bathroom. Mrs. Robins is Mrs. Trimnell's daughter in law's sister, & she is taking John, because Mrs. Trimnell had scalded her foot some time ago, it is so bad now, that she is in bed, & has to have medical attention. I should like Daddy to write a letter Mrs. Trimnell, & to ensure that there are no mistakes I shall enclose a letter which would be suitable. I think that although John has not been very well put up there, having had to sleep with the lodger, it can be understood that she must keep lodgers, as they are her only source of income, & as she is sixty-eight, you can imagine, how tired she is after looking after six person, & doing their washing. She had evacuees since the beginning of the war, & considering her age, strength, & financial position & livelihood, she has done very well indeed, & has done more that her share of National Service in helping evacuees, as there are many people in the town who are richer & younger than she, keep a maid & have no children & yet they refuse to have evacuees. I think that she deserves your appreciation & a letter is the best you can do to show that to her.

I think you ought to be satisfied with the number of cards & letters I have been sending lately, & I should like to have some replenishment for the money I am spending on stamps, & other things. We had 2/5 to share after spending a 1d on the postcard, & out of my 1/2½ I spent 2½d on milk, 4d on Scouts, 1d on stamps & have 4½d left, out of which about 2½d will go to-night on stamps. I do not know how John spent his share, & I do not know how much he has left, but I know that it is not much, so please send more. This Saturday I must get 5/4d worth of laundry (3/5½d last week) & we should like to cycle to Trowbridge or Chippenham to go to the pictures or go to the pictures here, if it is raining. Please send the money in the form of a postal order, because if you send cash I am liable to be fined.

There is not much more news otherwise, as nothing happened since my last card. However, here is a suggestion as to what Daddy might write to Mrs. Trimnell:-

'Mrs. Trimnell
4 Church Walk
Melksham, Wilts.
Dear Mrs. Trimnell,

I feel that I should not miss the last opportunity of thanking you for your efforts in making John happy, and putting him up to the utmost of your ability.

No one appreciates it more than I do, that, if John had not been quite comfortable, for having to sleep with a lodger, it was because that was the only way you could manage to feed him and yourself from your mean billeting allowance. Apart from this, the fact that you had evacuees since the war started, at your age, & financial means, is very praiseworthy indeed, & it can safely be said, that you have done more than your share of the National Effort and have done it remarkable well indeed.

I have been extremely sorry to hear o[f] your scalded leg, and I sincerely hope, that you will soon be much better, and be restored to your former health and vigour. At the same time I do wish to apologise for the extra work & inconvenience that was put on you through John, and to than[k] you for managing so well, and really I am glad that you are now relieved of this extra worry.

Hoping that your foot will be better soon
I am, yours sincerely,
(signature)'

Do not think that this letter is exaggerating Mrs. Trimnell's merits, & I am sure that she will be very proud when she receives it, to have gained so much of your satisfaction. About a fortnight after John is moved I should write another letter to Mrs. Robins thanking her for giving John shelter, & how happy he is there etc. People expect these thanking letters.

I shall leave room for John on the other side.

With love from Andrew

… continued by John on the back

Dear Mum and Dad,

We have very good news, I shall be moved on Saturday. I might go to the Vicarage and I might go to somewhere else. But I am sure I shall be moved.

I have not received my watch please send it.

Lots of love,
from John

The Wonders of a Semi-detached

This semi-detached on an estate of identical houses boasted a bathroom and toilet downstairs. A very knowing girl, their daughter Ruby was a year younger than me. Three years my junior was their son Michael, with whom I shared a bed. He would later press his face to the frosted glass bathroom window from outside and shout, 'I can see your black brush,' when I stood up in the bath.

Now aged 12, I was becoming ever less inadequate in the nether regions and ever more conscious of the subsequent stirrings – these led to matching a past neighbour Gerald's prowess and also gained Michael's admiration. The bathroom afforded the privacy to explore, experiment and finally to enjoy the exciting discoveries that followed. I had heard of a mysterious white fluid that passed into a woman's tummy and often wondered how anybody could know its colour, as it passed directly from inside a man to inside a woman. Now I knew – almost.

Marigolds grew around the front garden, while the back garden was completely cultivated with vegetables. The government's 'Dig for Victory' inducements meant that most people grew their own vegetables and our school provided kids with their own allotments; on mine I grew everything I could sell. A large marrow carried a mile or two would fetch a worthwhile couple of (old) pence.

The fields behind provided endless rambling opportunities among tall hay and wildflowers, backing onto fields close to Andrew's billet whence I had been so summarily expelled. Before he returned to London on passing his 'Matric' exams, and while he was quarantined with the mumps, I was unable to bring him the weekly issues of *The Hotspur*, *The Champion* and *The Adventure*: 'two-penny bloods' we both assiduously read. Here, the semaphore signalling we practised at Scouts provided the way to keep him up to date, as we stood on opposite sides of a great meadow and I transmitted the latest adventures of Rockfist Rogan in his 600mph sabre-nosed rocket fighter, which cut the wings off German planes, and how Windy Jones was getting along with the snobs at his highfalutin boarding school.

Charlie Robbins, the father, was away in the army, where he was a cook, and his rusting bicycle languished in the shed, un-ridden, till I could persuade Mrs Robbins – Maud – to let me clean it up and use it. At last, I could ride around Melksham with the other boys and, instead of cadging a bike for the five and a half miles to the Trowbridge swimming baths, I could ride 'my own'. When Charlie was invalided out of the army and worked at the RAF 'Camp' as a navvy, my pedalling freedom ended and I was back to cadging again. More accident prone on foot than on a bike, I slipped on the Robbins' front path and broke my forearm into a nice curve. The day my plaster was cut off I fell on it again. Hearing the ominous crunch, I walked the mile to the hospital, where an unbelieving sister put it in a sling and sent me home. After several painful weeks, mother took me to Charing Cross hospital during a visit home. I was mystified by the roars of laughter from the medical students surrounding the doctor attending me, when this 12-year-old Scout complained how a stupid Sister had tested his arm for crepitus, to check if my 'green stick fracture' had been re-broken. Another few weeks in plaster left me with a strong – if still slightly bent – forearm.

Maud Robbins banned us children from the sacrosanct, linoleum-covered front room, which was reserved for visits from better-off relatives. Instead we spent all of our indoor time on the hard chairs round the kitchen table, where we listened to the wireless. Week in, week out, without variation, Sunday dinner (really lunch) was roast beef and Yorkshire pudding, with (only ever boiled) potatoes. Cold cut leftover beef on Monday was followed by corned beef on Tuesday, my favourite 'Zoop' stew Wednesday, sausages Thursday and lamb chop Friday. I was sent out for the fish and chips on Saturdays. Sunday's pudding was invariably prunes and custard, when Charlie counted out the prunes as he served one at a time onto our plates in turn. He was responsible for baking the weekly cake, evidently the result of his army training.

A lot older than Charlie, Maud Robbins was really stepmother to Ruby and Michael. Thin and scraggy, she was easily agitated. When wearing her Sunday-best clothes, which on such occasions included a corset, her normally absent bottom took on a curiously square shape. An 'egrivating'

Charlie and Maud
Robbins. (By kind
permission of
Michael Robbins)

good-for-nothing, I only had to knock the handle off a jug for her to fly into a rage and, leaping out to the back doorstep, lift it high over her head and smash the offending remains into a thousand pieces with apparent relish. Then to my incomprehension, with venom she would invite me to 'go have a deep one', after which she would feel better.

I managed a couple of weekends to London by hitching a ride with local overnight lorry drivers for two 'bob', and for an 12-year-old it was wonderful to see the dawn en route – without any thought or fear about safety in the care of a stranger. Mother awaited my arrival on the street corner, wearing a worried frown – I didn't know why. She would have had more cause to worry later, had she known how I was taken to the 'rec' and beaten up by three bigger boys, for letting on about their thieving at W.H. Smith.

By then I was well on through puberty and growing fast – though so were these older thugs. To my satisfaction, I was no longer in a position to be humiliated, as when two years earlier one of my 13-year-old tormentors had shamed me in the boys' lavatories by comparing his superior penis with mine. 'What d'ya think you've got there? Now this is a prick!' Nip Reese boasted, hanging it out for me to admire. When I reached 13, the big thrill was Dad shaving the thick growth of hair off my upper lip when I visited home.

13 *March 1940*

Dear Mum & Dad,

I hope you will not faint, receiving a letter so soon after the last one, but the matter is urgent, because there are so many people booking seats for the 11.19 bus on Thursday that I am afraid that we cannot get seats unless you send the 12/- down as soon as you get this letter. I tried to reserve 2 seats, but I was told that I must pay straight away. I should be glad to receive 1/- extra for a school cap. I think you will understand, that if I cannot get the seat on that bus, the I shall not arrive till later in the evening, or have to go by train which cost 16/- instead of 12/- for two of us. So please, as soon as you get this letter (first post to-morrow, I hope) post 12/- by telegram if possible, so that I can book the ticket to-morrow or Friday the latest. Even Friday might be late. From the wireless I understand that you received letters from the Ministry of Health & the Board of Education – not to bring us back for the holidays, but do not worry about that, it is nonsense.

The situation regarding John is unchanged. I have some more marks available, they are; French – 90%; Shorthand 96%; Book-keeping 79%; Arithmetic 86%; General knowledge 64%; Scripture 50%; Geometry 100%; Composition 85%; Average 86%. Total 510 out of 600. I am top in every one of the subjects mentioned here, and I have the history, english & algebra results to come yet.

Lots of love from
Andrew

Dear Mum & Dad,

Before turning to slightly more unpleasant subjects, I should like to offer you my best wishes for your coming wedding anniversary on the 5th inst. May God give that you will have a much happier year than the last one, & that we might all soon be together, & that Daddy's business might take fortunate turn, that we shall all live a happy & long life together. May the Lord God free you from all worries & troubles, illness & sorrow, & let him fulfil all your ambitions & desires.

I am sorry to say that I have no money to buy you anything, even so much as a flower or a small souvenir for the occasion. However we may almost assume, that or arrival to London next Friday or Saturday, will be a present, even thought you will have to pay the postage in advance.

I cannot understand why you complain as to lack of news from us, as I only received about two letters from you in the past fortnight, & if anybody, it was me who ought to complain. I do not only write when I want something, only if I'd want it, then I mention it in the letter. If I have only been writing postcards that was because John spends about 6d a week on 2d books, & on that come sweets & pictures, so that I have not much money left, as even with reasonable economy, money goes like a flash – think you have experienced that yourselves. Will you please forward my enclosed letter to Zsuzsi[17] for the occasion of her birthday, as I do not know the address. I shall write to Grandfather too, for his birthday.

There is not much news, since my last card, everything is the same every day. I have a lot of homework, writing letters, or if not that, then helping with gardening. If I do not do any of those, then John expects me to go out for a ride or walk with him, so life in Melksham is pretty monotonous. That is the reason why we go to pictures once a week.

I have been going to Synagogue (or rather a service) quite regularly since Pessach. I did not go on Tuesday morning, because it was raining hard. Both of us have been keeping to Matzo quite regularly during the eight days, & it was a relief on Tuesday night to have bread for supper.

Rosemary has got a slight touch of mumps, & I asked in school what I was to do, & I was told to go the same as usual. I very nearly came home on Wednesday morning, I already had my things packed, because of that. Now I am gargling, just to safeguard against infection, but I so not think that any harm will come.

Talking of harm, I quite agree with you that it was silly of us going in the open-air baths. I did not want to go in but John insisted, but I should not have gone in if I had known how cold the water was. It was only the water that was too cold, not the weather. Had the water been warmer, we should have been able to have a very nice swim. Anyhow, we cam out quickly & had a cup of tea at the canteen, but that did make much difference, – we were still shivering so much that we could scarcely hold our cups, & when it started raining, we went in & dressed. I dare say it will be very nice there in July – by the way tell Noni not to lecture about that swimming, otherwise I am not coming home for Whitson.

You need not send money for laundry this week, as I was too late for it, & it will only be ready next Saturday, & then I shall be in London. On the other hand, I shall soon want toothpaste, soap & lost my comb, so send very nearly the usual amount. Then I suppose I shall have to give half of it to John for his sweets & comics, & buy stamps & soap etc. on the other half. I do not think that it is fare that John should have all the pleasure out of the money, & I should buy all the necessaries. Even for this stamp, John wants me to borrow 2d from Mrs. Kelly, because he wants a comic to-morrow & he will not give me 2d for a stamp, when he ordered the comic. So for goodness' sake send us some money by Saturday morning, so that John might have his comic otherwise he will kill me.

There is no need to worry about John's bicycle, as he does not go outside the town without me, & he is careful, & the bike is in a better condition than mine. I do not like the idea of seeing the other boys with nice new sports bikes, & me a piece of old iron that rattles. I could easily spend £2 on renovating the bike, – but still I have given up the hope of getting a proper bike for the next year or so.

I am glad to hear that Daddy got his permit, & that he can get employment, if he finds a suitable job. I wonder if that applies to me as well.

Italy seems to be on the verge of entering the war with Germany – I never expected this.

I am leaving room for John too!

Lots of kisses, best wishes & love,
from Andrew

P.S. Did you know that Magyari, the Hungarian Gypsy died a few days ago?

3 May 1940

Dear Mum and Dad,

I wish you all the best of luck for your wedding anniversary, may it be granted that you shall live a very happy long and healthy life, and let us hope that we shall be together again.

Thank you for sending my watch. When it arrived it had a broken glass, we had it mended and was all right, but after a few days it kept stopping and now it wont go at all and the winder is broken off.

When I read Andrews letter I was really very disappointed that he even envies me for buying 3, 2d books a week and a little sweets (Andrew bought some too, so he can't say anything). And I think it is really mean that when we get 6/- and I have 1/6 while Andrew has 4/6 that I cant spend the 1/6. Andrew has too many necessaries, it is not my fault either if he looses his comb.

Lots of love to Noni, Mariska and you
John

23 May 1940

Dear Daddy,

I got your letter to-day and I was very pleased with it, but you were a little absent minded as you wrote that you were sending some money but you forgot to put the money in. We are breaking up for our Witsun holliday next Friday 30/5/41. Please send the fare to go to London and some money for myself <u>at once</u>, as you have not sent me any at all yet. I am longing to meet you all. How is business? I am glad Andrew has got a nice new suit, and I hope to get one too.

I have got a fairly bad caugh. I hope to see you soon, and Mummy Andrew Noni & everybody. I[s] Vera still in London? I am short of news so I must say good bye. Hoping to see you soon.

Lots of love and kisses from your everloving son,
John

11 June 1940

Dear Mum & Dad,

I received your last letter on Friday & I am sorry I am so slow replying. Even then I cannot put a stamp on as I am absolutely and perfectly broke. Of course that does not matter much as long as you know it.

First of all I want to convince you that your assumptions – that it would be silly to camp in an open field where there are no shelters – is entirely incorrect and erroneous. Of course, when you are in a town with lots of houses and buildings, then if an air-raid occurs, your best policy is to stay in the house or go to a shelter and then you will be protected from flying glass and debris. In the country, however, the best thing to do is to go out into a field – far away from houses and be on the ground. Then you will not be hit by glass or debris. That is the reason why they make trenches in open places such as Hyde Park.

We shall be camping (if you do not want us to go alone, we need not except when we are on a Troop or Patrol camp) in a field like that, where we shall be safer than anywhere else from aerial attack. It is doubtful whether a German bomber would waste bombs on an open field. The tents will be camouflaged so as to be invisible from the air, & so – if you refer to the cruelty of German airmen who machine-gun women and children – he will not even spot us. If where is a direct hit near us, it does not matter whether we are in a town or in the country or in a field, it will finish us off. THE CHANCES ARE THAT WE ARE LESS LIKELY TO BE HIT IN AN OPEN FIELD where there is no object in bombing or machine-gunning than in Melksham or any other places. Besides do you imagine that the Scouting authorities and the Ministry of Home Defence would permit camping if it was unsafe! Camping is prohibited within a certain radius of military objectives as I can safely say that we shall not be attacked & we are safer in the fields than in town.

Up to now I have explained why you should not forbid me to camp. Now I shall say why it is important that you should send me camping, not keep me at home, as you know, my physique is weak, & I need as much open air, sunlight and exercise as I can get hold of, & I should never miss a chance of strengthening my muscles, expand my chest, & making me look more like a champ. You know that whenever I came back from camp I looked healthier & better than ever. Besides it will relieve the monotony of country-life, & of swotting for the Cambridge & it will give me a better chance to get on more friendly terms with other boys – another very important factor in my after-life. You know very well that you cannot get on without any friends, & I have no real friends up to now in the true meaning of the word. As a Patrol Leader, my presence is almost essential at a camp to set good example to other boys, to gain experience and to instruct recruits from the experience & knowledge I have gained.

The camping ground is only 3½ miles from Melksham so we can cycle there in about 20 minutes at the most. I hope I have convinced you upon this point so I ask you to write saying that you give me &

John permission to camp any time during the camping season, signed by one of you. THERE IS NO NEED FOR UNEASINESS OR ANXIETY on the matter as the Scoutmaster & other Scouts are quite proficient in A.R.P. [Air Raid Precautions] & first aid, the two factors which are most important nowadays. Remember this when you want to argue from the point of view that there are no shelters to protect us. – The use of shelters is for protection from flying glass & debris. In an open field far away from houses, glass & debris cannot reach you. In Melksham, there are no shelters that would protect you from direct hits so you are safer in the fields.

By now you will have heard that Italy declared War on us, & I am just hoping that Hungary will keep out of it until she is invaded by Germany & she comes in with the allies. Otherwise I think it will only help us defeating Germany for Italian troops are not much good. I daresay in a few weeks time Mussolini will find it safer in Abyssinia than in Rome.

Please send some money as soon as you can because I have the laundry to get out (2/8) & we have no money. There are other things to buy too, such as a new spoke for the bike John is using, & my tyres will not last long either.

I am afraid John cannot write on this letter because he is in school. I am going on Thursday.

Lots of love from,
Andrew

Dear Mum & Dad,

I am afraid I cannot be quite as prompt in my reply as you might have expected, because the matter of reevacuation naturally wants a great deal of consideration & I admit that I have not yet come to a conclusion & I have had no adequate chance to speak to a master yet.

However, here are my arguments. Naturally it would be hard for all of us to be separated for such a long time, but if other things point to the fact that it would be more advantageous for us to forget the sentimental side of the question then we shall drop that. Of course it would be a grand thing to go overseas for a short time especially to the U.S.A. In fact I should ask you to consult Uncle Arthur[18] on the matter. But another more important question is, how will it affect our education! I shall be sixteen in December so I shall probably have to come back then, & I doubt if John would want to stay there any longer whereas I do not see how he could come back, since you sent him to be safe. My Cambridge studies will have to be interrupted, & I do not know whether it would not ruin my career if I did not get that, as you cannot get very far without some qualification as the Cambridge, Oxford or Matriculation. Naturally it would have a good effect if I could see something of the New World, but am I not too young to go & 'see the world'? I think that the time for that will come when I shall have finished my home education & shall be called Dr. Andrew Forbat.

Another point for which we might not be eligible in that we are not British subjects. They can only take a limited number at a time & the first 20,000 has been over applied for. I rather think that they will consider British boys' applications first, & by the time our turn might come I shall be sixteen.

I shall not say whether I want to go or not. It is a question of is it better to stay or go. Certainly it would be adventure, fun, new experience & friends, but on the other hand I might lose valuable education & a career of a lifetime. The other two factors are more of safety, & sentimental feeling. I leave you to balance all these up one against the other & decide.

We had an air-raid warning last night when a south west town was raided, but no bombs were dropped in or near Melksham & I think it was a waste of time staying under the stairs, for two hours. I bet Granny was excited when the sirens were sounding in London.

I endeavour to post the letter tomorrow which a few lines from John & do not be cross for being slow to reply.

The winder of my watch fell off & I took it in. It will cost me 3/6. Besides, my bicycle tyres are really worn through, & they will cost me in the neighbourhood of 5/6. It seems to me that I shall have to try & get a part time job outside school-hours, with your permission of course.

With lots of love from,
Andrew

2 July 1940

Dear Mum & Dad,

Thank you very much fo[r] your last letter, & as I was disappointed in the 'enclosure', I am afraid this will have to be an 'expensive' letter.

I have not got the job of taking the paper round but I shall try with the milk, or other before-school jobs. I must earn a few shillings a week, because I very badly need new tyres for my bike, as they are so worn-out that I get a puncture every other day.

I have had a very pleasant time at camp last week-end. Mrs. Kelly gave me 2/6 as my share towards buying the food, otherwise I could not have gone. This week-end I hope to go to a Patrol-Leaders' Camp at Lacock, & after that John will be able to come with me every time.

I thank you for the advice about air-raids – of course we should not have been looking out of the windows anyhow. From now on, I ask you to carry your gasmasks all the time. In my opinion, the Germans are likely to invade us any hour now, & I think that one of their methods of creating panic will be by gas. You must be prepared for real mass air-raids on London too, as they will hope to cause as much confusion as possible. Very likely, they will come from the West by aeroplane, because they will not expect to find so much resistance there. Be prepared, however and whichever way they strike, and follow the instructions on your leaflet 'If the invader comes' carefully. Have you cleared the office of inflammable materials? Did you tell your neighbours about putting out fires caused by incendiary bombs? Do you know how to use a stirrup-pump? If I were you, I should see your warden about these matters.

I am afraid it would be impossible for us to come down to London now. I have already missed a great deal through my mumps, & I am stilly busy catching-up. I could not afford to come down now. Besides, we are faced with the most critical weeks of the British Empire, & I think it would be to our mutual advantages if, for the time being, we should stay-put. What about you coming sown to see us though!

I have just heard (3-7-40) that instead of summer holidays, we shall have Mondays & Fridays off throughout July.

We shall have no P.L.s' camp this week-end – but we might go camping all the same. The trouble is that the six-form boys (for only they are going this week-end) do not want John to go with them. But I shall do my best to persuade them.

Well I shall leave off now, to post the letter. I am afraid it always takes come time to get a letter finished & posted. If you can please send my tent down. Don't forget to put money in the next letter, & please write two notes (one to Mr. Redfearn & one to the Scoutmaster) that you give me permission to be A.R.P. messenger.

Lots of love from,
Andrew

13 July 1940

Dear Mum & Dad,

Thank you for the letter & the money inside it. (Not for the grumbling about not writing).

I am afraid I have a bit of bad news but don't worry. John fell on his arm while running and split the radius and the ulna (two bones in the forearm). John was playing on Thursday night, & while running, he slipped on a bit of wet wood. I[t] was all out-of-shape, & John thought it was dislocated. He went straight to Dr. Campbell, who told him to go to the hospital at 10.30 a.m. At the hospital he had two X-ray's taken & the Doctor found that it was broken. He put it in plaster (gipsz) & then applied a large arm sling. HOWEVER, PLEASE DON'T worry, he did not even cry when it happened – it does not hurt much, & the situation is far from serious, in fact it is quite a lucky accident ('But it's not a proper fracture' – shouts John) – hence can you see that he is all right.

I had my first wages today, together with your 2/- however, result of day's spending leaves me with 2½d. Here – my statement of account – all important items:-

tyre	3/3
inner tube	1/-
soap & toothpaste	8
toothbrush	1
debts paid	9
	5/9
John's books	4
stamp	2½ = 6/3½

– balance = 2½ as stated.

So please, as soon as you can in your next letter, send us something if only 1/-, because I owe Mrs. Kelly 3*d* for a broken plate, & Mr. Kelly 3*d* for a pump-connector.

By the way, I did receive the parcel.

Please send the money for going home soon, because I want to book my seat a week in advance (14/-).

My trousers look more like a piece of rag, because it is in pieces (more or less) so please send Uncle Eugene's old trousers, & John's watch, cub hat & Jersey, because he wants to give it to Mrs. Robbins (most likely she will give John a few shillings for it).

With lots of love,
Andrew (& John)

P.S. John cannot write, his right arm being in plaster. And DON'T worry !!!!!!!!!!!! A.

6 September 1940

Dear Mum & Dad,

I have not had any letter from you since Friday, & I should like you to write more often, especially as there are a lot of air-raids in London & in view of the numerous casualties, it causes me some anxiety with regard to your safety if I have no information for a considerable period of time.

My work is increasing daily, as there are only 11 more weeks to go before the exam & I have to do a great deal of revision & new work in order to get through. The fee is 35/-, & we were told to-day to get it ready, because the applications for the entry will soon have to be sent in.

In spite of the fact that I had 4/6 wages on Saturday, I have only a few coppers left, as John spent 1/1 at Weston (out of his watch money), & I had to pay Mrs. Kelly 1/3 for doing the laundry (saving of 1/6 on the laundry price) & I also bought a 6½d box of chocolates for her birthday. Apart from that I bought 4 periodicals, haircream, pencil sharpener, rubbers, notebook & a small amount of sweets. It is terrible how quickly money goes, & I should be obliged if you could send some more.

John says that he needs some socks badly, as Mrs. Robbins is complaining about the enormous holes & the thinness of the socks. Can you send him about 3 pairs!

Just to answer you that there are no air-raids & then to close my letter, because I have lots of work to do to-night yet.

Lots of love from
Andrew

15 September 1940 – a postcard

Dear Mum & Dad,

Sorry I am late in replying to your card (dated the 9th, received the 12th) but as you might guess I am very busy lately.

Please try to write to me as often as you can, & write details about the raids because from what I hear from Billy Childs, who is here for the weed-end, quite a number of bombs were dropped in his district which is not far from ours.

John had the plaster taken off & his arm is still a little stiff. It is very quiet down here so do not worry.

Please send me money if you can. I put 1/6 in the savings & spent nearly all the rest of my wages, as I went to the 1/- seats in pictures with John (the 6d being horrible & as I went with my friends). I shall soon have to give up my paper job because of the intensity of homework, but I cannot do that unless I am assured of a regular pocket money. Hoping that you soon receive good news from the B.B.C. & that you are all right.

Lots of love from
Andrew
and John

John's original postcard of 15 September 1940. (Author's collection)

Notes from Father

In those days, the war, which for a year had been a 'sleeping war', began with full force. Hitler invaded Belgium, Holland and France and within days swept away the resistance. The British were forced to withdraw their forces from France and the French gave themselves over to Hitler without any real resistance. Even their government backed Germany. In Britain the helpless government was swept away and Churchill, who did not compromise, became the leader of Coalition Government. I had hardly started working in the Pop Inn when the Germans began their aerial bombing of London. Somehow, it left me cold; I did not feel the danger. Shelters were built all over London. One night the bombing was so heavy, that Mum wanted to go into one of the street shelters. Her mother, who was terribly frightened, had not slept at home for days, but in a shelter in a nearby house. The weather was turning cold and despite blankets, which we brought with us, we were very cold, so we did not go down any more. A Hungarian friend of Uncle Eugene, who lived with us, was so frightened that he asked if he could stay in our bedroom while the bombs were dropping. One evening I went out into the street with him. I amused myself by watching his fear at every explosion. Your sweet Mum could barely wait for me to return to the house. We began to hear of more and more fatal incidents.

Uncle Eugene offered Mum the job of cashier, and as he offered an additional £1, this meant a considerable increase in our livelihood and especially that once more we could spend the whole day together, made us very happy. From early morning to late in the evening we were working, having lunch and dinner together again without expense and that made the morning to night, seven-day work-week hard work tolerable. At night we could hardly get home because of the bombs dropping. There were always explosions around us. Houses collapsed, burying the inhabitants. We used to run from the shop to the Underground and then from Notting Hill Gate station to our home, listening to the engines of the planes overhead.

Meanwhile, I received an invitation for an examination at the BBC. I had to translate from German to English and the other way round, take an intelligence test, and they examined my capabilities and knowledge base.

After a long wait I got a notice that I passed and they put me on the waiting list. They would notify me if they needed me. I waited day by day with an anxious heart for their call; in the meanwhile I continued to work with greater strength and resolve at the Pop Inn. Sometimes the bombing was so severe that we could not go home. The Pop Inn had a basement restaurant and a basement passage and sometimes we spent the night there together with some of the other employees. We had a mattress there; Mum and I lay there arm-in-arm and slept like that. Sometimes her mother came in and slept with us.

In the restaurant, we started a so-called shelter-breakfast, which we served at 6 a.m. That was when people would emerge from the underground tunnels, where they hid from the bombs. At about 9 a.m., when breakfast was over and they began to clean the restaurant, we went home for an hour to bathe and change clothes, since we slept fully clothed. Gradually the restaurant got going, expenses diminished and income increased, but our wages did not rise. It was not sufficient to settle debts and the landlord seized our furniture. It looked as though we could not save the furniture, they would be auctioned, but the flat counted for little to us. You children were in the country and we were in the business all day.

Meanwhile we had other losses. We had to close the front door of the restaurant at night and we had to open the door under the gateway, which had to be covered with a curtain so as not to allow any light to get out. The door was next to the cash desk and in the cash, Mum had your beautiful crocodile handbag, which I had bought her back in Budapest. In it there was a gold cigarette lighter, with her monogram engraved, also bought in Budapest, as well as a little money and other small things. It was stolen by someone. Her heart was aching for them, but of course we could not even think of replacing them. I was in the habit of arranging the money and putting it into an envelope at the end of the day. Shortly after that the takings in the cash register were also stolen. It was not a big sum, but it was worth three weeks of my wages and I had to pay it back, so I got no pay for three weeks. I was getting used to these mishaps. Mum and I belonged to each other and that made up for everything in the world.

One evening, we were very tired and we wanted to go home to sleep in our beds. The bombing was so heavy, that we could not go out in the street.

When we went home in the morning to bathe and change, we found our house in a terrible state. Most of the surrounding houses were in ruins. The street received a direct hit. In our house all the windows and doors were ripped out. The bed on which we were to sleep was covered with broken glass an inch high, with the shards and splinters from the doors and windows. God knows what would have happened to us if we had slept in them. It was a lucky escape. Since we could not live there any longer, we informed the bailiff that we have to take our furniture. He said he would have them taken for auction and, he would save for us whatever could be saved. He offered us and your grandmother the use of his own house, where he would give us a couple of rooms cheaply. He charged more than we had paid (rent) for the whole house. It was a very cold and uncomfortable house. He said that we would get our bedroom furniture back; they could not auction that according to law. He would also save the armchairs and sofa, a very attractive set, for us. It was only a matter of £40–£50. He explained that if the furniture were auctioned, then we would not have to pay the arrears, which we had for the furniture; that was the law and we would come out well from this. He was so pleasant and polite and seemed so helpful that we trusted him. Next day we moved to his house with our stuff.

You children surprised us with another visit. As much as we feared for you because of the bombing, we were that much happy to have you with us for a few days. We could not stop delighting in you. You had grown – and become British. One afternoon you went to visit your Aunt Edith's family. The bombs were falling and you were not back in the Pop Inn. Mum could not bear the excitement and I was also anxious, but tried to calm her. Finally after another two hours, the phone rang. Then Mum at the nearest Underground station, and with wisdom and foresight she awaited a lull in the bombing. You children, especially Johnny, definitely enjoyed the thrill of the bombing and as we were sitting in the cellar of the Pop Inn, having our dinner, whenever we heard a bomb fall, Johnny shouted, 'Come on'. Actually, it was not at all funny; each morning we read in the paper how many died as a result of the bombing.

Mum went to see the arbitrator to discuss the details of the auction and he assured her how much advantage we would get out of it. Johnny

A bombed London home after post-war restoration. (Author's collection)

*accompanied her and the arbitrator was so friendly, that he gave John half
a crown, which he accepted with no little pleasure. Soon you returned to
Melksham, and we were glad that you left the most dangerous zone. The
difficulties with pocket money had eased, as now we could send a few
shillings and secondly because you both began newspaper delivery every
morning and were able to earn a little. Our poor boys had to get up at six
o' clock in the morning to deliver the papers before the start of school. We
were very proud of you that you were earning money and besides they were
among the teachers' most favoured students and the best pupils in their
classes. The children who went to the free school were usually of weak
social standing, because only poor families sent their children to a free
school. Nonetheless, as the future showed, you were excellent boys.*

    *It was a pleasant little apartment in West Kensington, with two modern
rooms, central heating, hot water in the bathroom, and an attractive little
kitchen. In one room they left the furniture, carpet and lamp, which we
took over and paid for later. We got our bedroom back except for the suite
of chairs, which was retained by the arbitrator for his own use. I could
not go to the auction because Uncle Eugene did not let me out of the Pop*

Inn, saying that there was no sense in going, seeing that I could not buy anything without money. The result was that the arbitrator told us that we could only have the £40–£50 if he bought the armchairs and corresponding sofa, not to mention the other furniture which cost several hundred pounds when we bought them. He consoled me by saying that at least I did not have to pay the remaining debt for the furniture. We did not grieve much over our losses. We had a modest lifestyle, a pleasant little flat and your grandmother was happy to be able to sleep in the shelter in the basement of the house, where many other residents also slept. That was not for us! We slept in our comfortable bed and hoped that a bomb would not find us.

We left for work early in the morning and returned late at night – usually dead tired. As we were coming home one night, just as we stepped out of the Underground into the street, we heard the sound of a bomb dropping. I grabbed Mum's hand and ran with her to the nearest doorway. In her fright, she did not know whether to run forward or backward and I dragged her to the doorway. The moment we got under the doorway, a tremendous explosion shook us and we saw that the house on the other side of the road had been hit and was on fire, together with all the neighbouring houses. A stone fell from our hearts and we felt secure once again. We went to the flat and I went to the window to see what happened in the street. We did not turn on the light because the blackout curtain was not drawn. We heard another bomb falling and she shouted, 'Get away from the window!'. She dragged me away from the window by force and at that moment all our windows were broken. If she had not dragged me away, I would have been cut up by the broken glass. We thanked God that no harm came to us. We lay down in the cold window-less room and snuggling up to each other we warmed each other up as we went to sleep. We were without windows for two years; it was impossible to get glass and they stuck cardboard in place of the windows. Often at night, when we had to change at Earls Court from the deep Underground to the surface connection to West Kensington, we had to wait for the train under the stairway, because bombs were dropping and it was not safe to go outside on to the platform.

21 September 1940

Dear Mum & Dad,

I have not posted yesterday's postcard, so I am including it in this letter. Yesterday I received your letter & the 3/6, for which I thank you very much, & I must congratulate you on your lucky escape. It was indeed a thing that we should all be grateful for to the Almighty, that the bomb that fell outside the house was a delayed-action bomb & not a high-explosive one. I hope this will also be a lesson to you, & that you will not take any more chances like that. I hope that the damage has only been slight, & that even if all the windows will be blown in, you will have the consolation that they will never blow in again.

I am sorry to hear that Mummy has lost her job, but still I hope, that by the time this letter arrives, Daddy will get his job at the B.B.C. I shall hang on to my job for the time being, especially as I want a pair of football boots, & besides I want to save some money for Victory. I have already got 3/- in the savings, & I hope to increase that this week.

I do not know, whether you know that there are some Hungarian people living in Pembroke Road, their name is Zsötés. They have a little boy of 8 up Bowden Hill (Hocock) who has been evacuated at the beginning of the war, – then he could speak no English at all, & now he is forgotten all his Hungarian.

I am going to meet John now, & read him your letter, as I only saw him yesterday in the morning, before your letter arrived.

Lots of love from
Andrew

6 October 1940

Dear Mum & Dad,

I am sorry I could not write for such a long time, but I suppose you will see that I am very busy nowadays. But to-day I happen to have slightly less work to do.

I received the Cambridge fee on Friday with many thanks.

There is very little news to write about, because my daily time table is so very monotonous. School, paper-round, school, homework, bed, every day. We have been having exams for last week & to-day & am doing fairly well.

Yesterday Mr. Kelly took me out in the car blackberry picking.

I hope you are all right, & that now you are put up well to sleep somewhere I thought, that my best plan after December will be to get a job straight away, go to evening school & in a couple of years time, when we hope to be English citizens, I can get all the Scholarships that I need for any course that I want to take. I shall only be 18 then & still have plenty of time, by then, I shall have some money saved up too & bear College expenses. I cannot afford t[o] pay any fees now & cannot get any Scholarships. Write & tell me what you think of it.

There is nothing else to write about, I shall get John to write again this week. Happy New Year (Roshashono was last Thursday & Yom Kipour will be on Saturday. I shall fast) & I hope it will bring more happiness than the last one.

Lots of love from
Andrew

14 October 1940

Dear Mum & Dad,

Thank you very much for your last card, which I received this morning. As you refer, to what will happen to us after December, I thought it might be as well to discuss the point in detail and make or plans the best we can.

Of course, there is no real problem if you are in Bristol. Then I shall get a good job there and save up sufficient money for some of the high school expenses. If, however you are still in London, as I hope you will not be, then I do not think it is advisable for me to go back to London, unless I am forced to. It is improbable that I can get a job in Melksham, but I might try and get one in Trowbridge or one of the neighbouring towns. Then however, the problem of lodging arises, for if I go to Trowbridge, then I shall have to get into somewhere for a sum which would nearly take up the whole of my wages. There is a great shortage of lodgings, and therefore the charge is high. Please consider these facts and decide.

We are quite all right, there are no air-raids, & I am busy, although not quite so busy as before. John has received his socks with thanks. He cannot write his letter because I am writing it in the dinner-hour, & have to post it before he can write.

Well I must get off to school now. So lots of love & luck

Andrew

P. S. Please send money, if you can.

9 November 1940

Dear Mum & Dad,

Thank you very much for your post card & letter to which, I am only able to reply now. I am afraid I have been rather busy, & now, 3 weeks before the examination I shall be busier still, so do not worry if the replies to your letters are slightly delayed as it is in this case.

To-day, I told Mr. Riddick[19] that I could no longer carry on with my paper round, since I had to stay up a little longer owing to increased home work & extra lessons & therefore it was impossible for me to get up early at the same time, & do my work efficiently. It had to be one or the other, but I could not do both. I know you will agree with me in this & even though you will have to send me money more frequently to supplement my wages. I know this will be hard on your pockets but it is only a matter of 6 weeks at the most.

You seem to be rather anxious to know if I am not overworking myself. Well I do not think you need worry a great deal about that, especially now that I have given up the paper-job.

It is true that I did not go to school yesterday because I did not feel too well in the morning, but after my paper round I went back to bed for the morning & I feel all right now.

I am afraid I have hardly had time to comment on your misfortunes up to now, since I only wrote short cards, on which I could only just write how we were going on, & what we were doing, & how broke we were. Of course I am sorry that you have so much work today & had to move so many times, but the main thing is that your are all right.

Mr. Redfearn told us yesterday that we have an alternative of three things after the Cambridge:-

(1) To go back to London

(2) Stay at School

(3) Get a job round here

I think I am going to ask him if I could get transferred to a Secondary School somewhere if I paid. It is probable that I could pay the fees from my paper-money but I shall have to ask about that. If this is impossible than I think I shall try to get a job somewhere in the neighbourhood which will supply me with lodging money & a few shillings pocket money & in the meanwhile I intend to get further education at an Evening School & then to be able to go on to a University when I can get Scholarships. I do not think it is advisable to back to London now, & I'd not want to stay on at Kelly's any longer than necessary, since they, I think they are planning to let the room in which I am now.

Well I cannot write any more, but I should like to have your views on the future. Please try to send money regularly, since I am sending my laundry out again & I have to save up for John's birthday present.

Lots & lots of love & millions of kisses from
Andrew

P.S. I have not got any thing for Granny yet, Mrs. Robbins is still full up. Shall I write letters to the West Kensington Court address – in Conan Street or to the bar?[20]

Dear Mum and Dad,

I am sorry I am writing with pencil today, but my fountain pen is in need of repair & it is a nuisance having to dip in the ink after every other word. I am afraid I am broke again & I should like you to send a little more this time, because I shall have to pay laundry, fountain pen, John's present, haircut, 6*d* I owe for John's haircut which he lost & my weekly expenditure. The total will come to nearly 9/-. Please send trousers urgently for both of us, because the ones we are wearing have big holes in the rear. John wants same size as last time & mine must be at least 40 inches from the hip to the shoes. Please send them quickly as we need them, & I want the money too! Please write, I have had no news from you for over a week. I must stop now, lots of love

from Andrew

29 November 1940

Dear Mum & Dad,

I got a bit fed up with swotting, having been at it for the last 2½ hours to-night, & so I am going to take a few minutes writing a nice & juicy letter to you at last.

We have had a very nice time at Mrs. Robbins's birthday, because she was nice enough to invite me for tea for John's birthday. We had white & brown bread, lots of jelly (two kinds) some small cakes & your birthday cake which was the best of all. Did Mummy make it herself?

Mrs. Kelly made an extra effort this time too, because apart from Rosemary giving John a little home-made leather purse, Mrs. Kelly gave me 1/- to buy something for John in Rosemary's name. First I bought him a Trix gear-set but on closer inspection with John I found that it was no use unless you had a decent size Trix construction set. We thought it would have been nice to have bought that on part of the

10/- but going back to the shop we found that they did not have any of those, so we gave the gear all back, & instead we told Mrs. Kelly's shilling as a contribution towards a 2/6 sheath knife. Mrs. Robbins also gave John a shilling for which he bought a bottle of haircream & a tube of toothpaste, & he also bought a 3*d* packet of 25 birthday candles (12 for this year & 13 for the next).

Please don't be cross with me for spending a lot of money, I am really doing my best, but the after the main expenditure, the laundry is paid & I gave something to John & buy the periodicals there is not much left out of 4/-. This time I had also to buy a 'Hotspur Book' got 3/- (I took that out of the savings) & from the first 4/- that you sent I gave quite a lot to John, bought periodical but although I have not been able to pay for my laundry (owing to lots of little expenditures such as haircuts & others I cannot remember) had 9*d* left when you sent John's money. To-day I spent 2/2 on my fountain pen & owe still another 2/2 for it, because they had to put a new nib in. John only gave me 2/- so I have 6*d* left after buying 1*d* worth of sweets. I say all this not to complain but to give you an idea, what a lot I spend & what a little I get for it & practically no pleasure out of my money. I dare say you yourself have experienced that money, especially in wartime. Still, after Xmas I intend to resume my paper-round & that will help to straighten matters out. How are you getting on financially now? I should like to know something in that respect.

I am terribly busy nowadays, & for example on Sunday I have been working ALL DAY & have not been out at all. I wish I could see you, for I miss you a lot. I shall be delighted to come down for a few days at Xmas & my birthday. I promise to stay down in the shelter during raids, & really it will be quite an experience. Besides we shall have plenty of things to talk about & discuss together. The only difficulty is what John will say & I should like you to explain to him by letter that it is not for him to go back.

My examinations are starting next Monday & will continue until Wed. Dec. 11th. In the meanwhile pray for my success – it will be hard going.

I hope that Mummy has recovered from the bad shock on that Friday night when 6 bombs were dropped round you. Still, I hope that you have a safe shelter to go to, & that you are getting a little sleep at night in spite of the rat. Cheer up & chin up!

Well, I cannot think anything more to write about so lots & lots of love & kisses from Andrew

P.S. I have not yet received the trousers, socks handkerchiefs & ties.

… continued by John

Dear Mum and Dad,

I thank you with all my heart for the 10/- and the cake. I bought a sheath knife and I've got 5/- in the savings, and a few other things I have not received the trousers etc. yet nor has Andrew. Mrs. Robbins invited Andrew to tea on Tuesday and she made two jellies and some fancy cakes. Are you all right? Have there been many raids? We are fine.

Lots of love from
John

5 December 1940 – in best copperplate handwriting

Dearest Mother,

Let me, first of all, wish you a long and very happy life for your birthday. May the God Almighty grant you very much better years in the future than the last few have been, and may we all live together in happiness for the rest of our lives. May you have nothing but pleasure from your children, who will always do their best to give it to you, and may sorrow and worry be kept far from you, and it is my earnest prayer that we may all live together happily, without worry and in health as long as it please the Almighty.

I am afraid I cannot buy you any presents, not even the seven stalks of red roses, that you so like. But as a mark of my love, I am sending you my birthday greetings in my best manuscript writing. (If I can so as well to-morrow for the manuscript writing examination then I shall not worry.)

I have a little good news for you, because up to the present I have done quite well in the examinations, and should get a credit in most subjects. Up to now we had or Book-keeping, English, Literature and Mathematics.

I am sorry to mention that there is bad news too. John's middle left fingernail had to be taken off yesterday morning, because it turned sceptic [sic] underneath. It turned rather bad during Tuesday night, and when, on Wednesday morning he went too the hospital about it, Dr. Spence & Dr. Woodhouse gave him gas and took his fingernail off. He was well enough to-day to go to school, but he does not look too well, and he could do with some tonic.

Well, lots of good luck and many, many happy returns from your loving

Andrew

… continued by John – also in best copperplate writing

Dear Mum and Dad,

I wish Mum many happy returns of the day. Let God let you have 100 years and more in happiness, health and comfort. I am sorry I have no mony to buy you anything this year and I hope that you will forgive me.

If Andrew comes home for Christmas and the air-raids are not too bad will you please let me go with him.

We received the trousers etc. on Friday the 29 tell Uncle Eugene that I thank him for the socks. And I thank you for the trousers they are warm.

I had to go up to the hospital yesterday as I have a septic finger. I was laid down on a bed and had gas to make me unconscious while they took my nail off as the septic part of my finger was right by it. The gas made me sick when I came home, so I went to bed that afternoon.

How are you getting on in the air-raids? I hope you are well. We've had a few warnings lately but nothing has happened.

Lots of love and 1000000001 kisses from your loving son
John

… continued by John – written in Hungarian

Dear Noni,

Thank you very much for the tie and the handkerchief they were very nice and I was very pleased with them. Do not be afraid of the raids. I hope that I shall see you soon. Was your birthday nice? Write and tell me.

I send 999999 kisses
Johnny

Undated – partially typewritten

Dear Mum and Dad,

In this letter I include the reports of the examination of October last, and the school has therefore contributed 1*d* to the stamp, thus saving some of my money as well as theirs.

However, talking of saving money, I am afraid that I cannot feel too pleased with myself for last Saturday I spent a monstrous amount on trifles, and I humbly beg your pardon for it. Namely I spent altogether 5/- on pictures, fares to pictures, and refreshments after pictures. It happened this way, because 'Pinocchio' was on at Trowbridge and I considered it to be such a work of art as what deserves a second look. So after spending 1/3 on fares for the two of us in a crowded bus, I found a huge crowd waiting outside the Gaumont, and it took us about an hour to get in. Then I found that the only seats below 1/10 left were the 1/6 ones, and what was worse there were no half price seats for John. After pictures we were rather hungry so at Woolworth's I bought 4*d* worth of biscuits. During my walk round Trowbridge (in order to recover Rosemary's lost gasmask at the Lost Property Office) I passed a sweetshop because John was very thirsty and he wanted something to drink (2*d*) and we spotted two 2*d* bars of chocolate, which are so scarce that I could not resist the temptation of buying one each. That very wonderfully and fearfully makes up the 5 Bob.[21]

I have received your letter and contents this morning for which I thank you very much and which rather eases my financial tension.

As regards further education, I saw Mr. Redfearn about it to-day, & he said that in his opinion my best policy was to wait in school until we get the results for the Cambridge, & then we can apply to a Secondary school for a transfer. However all the masters I spoke to about becoming a doctor warned me about high fees, long training & the necessity of cultivating a good 'bedside manner', which really the key to success for a good, successful & confidence inspiring doctor.

You will see from the reports that, just as you say, John's report is very unsatisfactory. He only came 21st in the class, & from the Schoolmaster's note below it is obvious that he is not satisfied either.

Well I cannot spare any more time, but I should just like to say that I miss you tremendously & I should like you to write to me just how things are in London, & whether it is a possible consideration that I should come down for a few days after the exam, for my birthday, which would give us a chance to talk things over.

Millions of kisses from
Andrew

(I am writing in pencil, because my pen does not work. I shall have to get a new nib.)

Growing Pains

Except on rare occasions, the only Melksham school had no room for 'the Londoners' so we were taught in a series of church halls spread around the town, involving a mile or so hike between lessons. After school, we were recruited to sweep acres of floorboards, employing large brooms and of buckets full of soggy used tealeaves, to keep the dust down. Brought back from retirement, elderly teachers well past war-service age – like rotund little Mr Foy – drilled French verbs into us and remonstrated with the help of hearty slap about the face when we got them wrong. Wispy white-haired English and history master Mr Bell, 'Dinger', had an unfortunate propensity to hit the wrong boy whenever some offending behaviour aroused him, usually resulting in whoever was nearest getting it in the neck. Rocking back and forth like one of those egg-shaped, pot-bellied, musical toy clowns, 'Nick' Redfern remonstrated in staccato time with his rocking, 'You have not done your homework!', while the big boys murmured *The Quartermaster's Stores* song: 'There was Nick, Nick, playing with his prick, in the stores, in the stores.'

Although two years younger than the rest of the class, I kept well up with the school work, which in a Central School included shorthand, touch typing and bookkeeping, that proved to be of considerable value in later life – but I was much chastened to be the only one still in short trousers. The others were so grown up and knowing about the ways of the world, with secret sayings and jokes whispered behind the hand that sounded intriguing – yet still much of a mystery to my innocent pubescence. I continued to hear the 'F***ing' word among other grown-up swear words, but I still had no clear idea of how it was done. It was definitely to do with girls, but as a good Scout, whose law said I had to be clean in thought and deed, and taught us to respect a girl's body, I made no efforts to explore the subject myself. Being as always the youngest and somewhat the outsider, my older 14- and 15-year-old friends' secretive 'any moment now' whispers were half-heard mysteries. Out in the fields, the 15- and 16-year-olds spent much of their time fervently

Melksham Baptist church. (Author's collection)

engaged in a seemingly pointless game called 'Kiss Chase' with girls, and I remained ignorant about their purpose.

Only having known girls who were my cousins – always older and wiser – my curiosity was not compelling enough to think of breaking the taboo associated with their superiority over little boys. Anyway, girls were sissy and a bit of a waste of time – especially Maureen Sullivan who seemed besotted by my disinterested presence next to her during the Saturday afternoon cowboy cliff-hanger movie in Melksham's tiny 'Picture Palace'. Lucky she was not there when I joined some friends in trying my first Woodbine cigarette near the front row. Instead of inhaling, I swallowed the smoke and soon threw up over the seats in front.

12 December 1940 – a postcard

Dear Mum & Dad,

Thank you very much for your card, thought it is rather plaintive. The 5/- was very useful and I already paid another 1/- for my fountain pen, got my laundry out, bought pencils and periodicals. I have just finished my English examination and yesterday I did literature and arithmetic while on Monday we had book-keeping. So far I have done quite well. We had quite a number of warnings lately but no bombs were dropped anywhere in the neighbourhood. I am glad that Daddy has again good prospects to get into the B.B.C. I hope he does by Xmas. I have seen Mr. Redfearn & he says that I should wait till the results of the Cambridge come out, than apply for a transfer.

Lots of love & luck from
Andrew

P.S. trousers have arrived & fit very well; chocolate too.

Dear Mum & Dad,

I have arrived quite safely with John yesterday, & there was quite a surprise for me when I got back because Mrs. K announced that she was going to let my room on Wednesday, & therefore I should have to sleep on a garden swing (I think you have seen it in summer) in another room (which incidentally will not be nearly as warm as the other one was).

Today I went to school & have spoken to one or two of the masters. Mr. Boughton thought accountancy was a very good profession to choose only of course it would mean a lot of work. But he thought it was hardly worth while for me to stay here until March 'working my time', because really I should not learn much & would only get out of practice, whereas if I went home as soon as I knew the results, then I could get into what I had to do in an accountants office straight away. In view of this and Mrs. Kelly's apparent unwillingness to retain me (she has been down to the billeting office to try & get me moved) I rather think it would be best for me to go home when I get my results out. I should like you to look out for advertisements in the meanwhile & try to see your Chartered Accountant & see if he has a vacancy.

Talking of advertisements, Mrs. Kelly says she saw an advertisement for the W.U.D. [Wiltshire United Devises] who have vacancies for boys between 16 and 17. I am not particularly interested. I don't know what you think.

Mr. Williams said that he thought that accountancy was an already overcrowded line but of course with sufficient energy it was quite possible to succeed. He suggested that it would not be a bad idea to write up to the Civil Service in Bath. The Civil Service of course is one of the best & safest jobs to get into which pensions, but I doubt if they take aliens. Shall I try?

I am afraid by buying my birthday present I put myself rather short of money because the Scout trousers cost 6/11. I also bought two cycle lamp batteries (11d each) & a bulb (4d); the two batteries so that I should have them working for some time, because I might not be able to get them later. Also I met a friend who treated me to pictures before Xmas & now was short of money so I gave him 6½*d*. Together with a 2*d* bar of chocolate I think this expenditure adds up to 6/11

> 2/2
>
> 6 ½
>
> 9/9 ½

and accordingly out of 11/6½*d*, and a 2½*d* stamp left
But of that I have to go to Trowbridge and have my photograph taken for the Police. That means that I shall probably have to borrow some money from John because the photographs might be expensive. Beside that I have not got my laundry out so try & send me some more money as soon as you get your wages because I really bought all these things out of my birthday money.

By the way, I went to the Police Station yesterday, & they took a few of my particulars, but they said they would want a lot more. Shall I give mothers date of birth as 1895?

With hundreds of kisses, & write soon please & tell me what you think of it all.

Hoping to be home soon I wish you luck from
Andrew

P.S. John cannot write on this letter, because I am posting it straight away so that it should get there in time.

Dear Mum & Dad,

Thank you very much for your beautiful English letters, which I received first thing this morning. I think that I already have sufficient to say that I can spend a 2½*d* stamp despite my financial plight.

This morning a police officer called at school & fetched me out, & there he took a few particulars. I asked a lot of questions & found that I am allowed to travel, taking care of protected areas, that they will apply for me to be able to stay in Melksham for some time, because Melksham is a protected area & also for the retention of my bicycle. They told me that they will want your passport immediately, & my photograph which I shall have taken this afternoon after borrowing some money. So do not forget to send the passport straight away.

At school I spoke to Miss Crampton, the girls' headmistress, & she said that apparently there is no chance for me to get a scholarship to a secondary school, but she strongly advised me to take up accountancy & in the meanwhile to study on at an Evening School.

Don't be too hard on the Kelly's. I can quite understand their point of view, since I really upset their plans by coming back. Last night I spent my first night outside the bedroom, & I slept on a sofa in the lounge. I arranged my blankets like at camp, & I was quite warm enough, & as comfortable as could be expected. They especially Mr. Kelly, seem to be trying to compensate me for the loss of my bed, by being extra kind to me & I get extra nice things to eat, & apart from that, Mr. Kelly gave me a beautiful Oxford dictionary, containing over 1400 pages, which should be must helpful.

Everybody seems to think that my best line to take is to come back to London & get a job at an accountant's office, thus gradually working my way up to become a Chartered Accountant. Of course the problem is whether I should get the job in London or in Evesham,[22] & when. But in London, at least I shall be certain to be able to go to some Evening Classes & until we move to Evesham, I shall more or less pay for my own keeping from my wages, so that the financial side does not really come into it. However, look up all the advertisements in the papers, & make inquiries.

I think then, that we can take [i]t for granted that I am coming home in a month or two, & finally leave school. You will not have to pay any fares this time, because on going home for good, the Government pays the fares.

I think I have dealt with everything important except money which I hope I shall receive more of, during the week-end.

The weather here, is cold, & we had quite a lot of snow, but now it is quite dry again.

Lots of love from
Andrew

P.S. We have a half-holiday this afternoon so I am going to Trowbridge.

… continued by John

Dear Mum and Dad,

We arrived safely on Sunday safe and sound. Mrs. Robbins was very pleased with the presents from the Co-op guild. We play with it every night I am just going to the school party and I hope to have a fine time.

How are you getting on have you had many warnings? We havn't had any warnings yet.

Lots of love and kisses from
John

P.S. [from Andrew] Do send me a lot of money, because I had to borrow 2/6 from Mrs. Kelly for the photograph & I shall have to pay 1/- for my registration book, & 1/10d for the laundry. Don't forget the passport.

Andrew

14 January 1941

Dearest Mum & Dad,

Sorry I am only replying to-day for the letter, 10/- & parcel which I received yesterday morning, but I could not do it because I had to go to be examined for my Musician badge at Scouts. I am glad to say that I passed it. The examiner said that I was quite promising, & that I ought to carry on & have a lot of practice.

I have not got a lot to write either. I paid all my debts & obligations, gave John 1/6 & have still got enough to pay for the rest of the week. One of the boys asked me if I'd like to go to Trowbridge with him to-night to pictures, but I do not know yet, if I am going or not. This afternoon we shall either have football, or we shall have to make speeches, but looking at the weather, it seems that we are going to play football.

I was wondering, if there was any particular point in staying on here until the results come out. After all I shall get the results all right in London as well. Really there is no need to wait any longer than for the Registration to be completed, & then come home. Mrs. Kelly has hinted to me yesterday that she would rather have me go back as soon as possible, & to-day she was rather annoyed because I did not take my blankets up from the lounge (where I sleep) to the lumber room. She forgot to take into consideration that I was already ¼ of a hour late for letting me sleep in the lounge at all contrary to all sanitary reasons, because a living room should not be used as a sleeping room. I did not start an argument, it would not have been worth while – I just swallowed. This was the first incident of this kind since I came back – Mr. Kelly continues to be nice. It is really Mrs. Kelly who is the greatest & stingier of the two.

Well I must close now because it is nearly school time, I am sorry that I have run out of ink & had to finish the letter in pencil.

John cannot add to this letter, because I am posting it straight away, so that it should reach you as soon as possible.

Thanks again for the 10/-, the passport & John's medicine & thousands of kisses from Andrew.

P.S. I hope the kisses will be real very soon. By the way, here is what I spent:-

Mrs. Kelly returned	2/6
Registration fee	1/-
Laundry	1/10
Gave John	1/6
Stamps	2 ½
Lent a boy	½
Balance	3/-
	10/6

18 January 1941

Dear Mum and Dad,

We have not heard from you since Monday and we are getting worried. Please write at once.

Have you heard from the B.B.C.? I will be very glad when you go to Evesham because if Andrew goes home I will be very lonely and I'll want t[o] see you more often.

I am having my medicine regularly. How are you getting on? I hope Mummie's tummy is all right. We are all right. We've had a few warnings lately but nothing has happened Andrew is now with me at Mrs Robbinses playing Lotto (tombola) and I will play in a minute. Write soon and please send some more money as Andrew spent nearly all of it on his 'necessities'.

Lots of love from
John

Dear Mum & Dad,

I am really getting worried, because although I wrote on Tuesday, I had no word from you, & it is already Saturday. I hope there is nothing seriously wrong with Mother's tummy, & that you are safe from air-raids. I am writing now regularly, & I want you to write as well.

I think that I shall be ready to come home next Saturday i.e. the 25th Jan. In the meanwhile I shall have to make various arrangements here, & I should like to have a reply to this letter <u>by return of post.</u> Firstly, I think it would be more convenience for me to travel by rail, rather than coach, because of the lot of luggage. The Government however, only pays coach fares because that is the cheapest, but I think it will be worth while the extra 2 or 3 shillings. Then again, I shall not be able to carry all my baggage, so there will probably be a charge for my extra luggage & my bicycle. In the meanwhile I shall let you know the exact charge for all these & acquire a big box into which I can put most things for sending away.

Talking of finances, I might as well give you a complete list of expenditures since my last letter. If I remember rightly I had 3/- left then:-

pictures and fares there	1/6
chocolate	3
school fund	1
periodicals	4
chips	2
John	<u>6</u>
	2/10

This morning I had 2*d* left but Mrs. Newman, our lodger gave me 6*d*, which I was reluctant to accept for doing some of her shopping. She is really extremely nice. Now I have 8*d*.

I have seen Mr. Redfearn yesterday, & he says that I shall have to go into an accountant's office, but most accountants want a premium, while learning, so try to find one who does not want a premium & give me a little pocket-money.

I want your reply immediately therefore whether I am to come home by coach or train and whether I should post or send my things in advance or bring them on the train that I am coming. I shall send you a list of what everything will cost so that you can send me the money.

Oh yes, and 1/2½ laundry that will be ready for me on Monday.

Well lots of love & kisses, & write & tell me whether everything is all right.

(999,999,999,999,999,999,999,999,999,999)² kisses until next Saturday.

Your Andrew (worried)

P.S. I shall have a bath now & then go to see John so that he should write too.

Andrew

Undated letter – written in Hungarian

My only ones,

I got your card this morning I was very relieved that Mummy is now well.

Yesterday afternoon, the Kellys went to the cinema and as I was at home alone, I tuned the radio to Budapest and was lucky because not only was there excellent reception of every word but it was a good programme and in any case it was nice of the Kellys to leave me alone and to come home just as the programme finished. When I turned on the radio, there was Gypsy music and this was the first occasion since a long time that I have heard such Gypsy music and I can say that I was convinced that Hungarian Gypsy music has the world's most feeling. József Cselenyi sang the most beautiful songs to the music of Tóni Lakatos and for the first time I felt that wonderful sensation that raises one's heart and spirit with lyrics which are also sad. Sometimes I nearly cried and afterwards I nearly danced to the merry music.

After the Gypsy music there was a 6 seconds of news, which I particularly noted from the propaganda viewpoint. It looks like the Hungarian radio, as far as is possible reports events in a neutral manner and has to report German propaganda. From this I know that, for instance, they referred to German newspapers regarding Churchill's Glasgow speech, without giving any opinion. They did not give any Hungarian opinion. Then an American chap repeated his opinion of new developments. They did not speak about the African front. I don't know what you think, but it looks to me that Hungary would very much like to be free of German influence.

After the sport results, there followed a very nice radio play and as I felt that it speaks to me, I briefly write about its contents.

It starts at a Hungarian countryside castle, where the Gentry together with servants awaits a son returning from America after three years away, with his wife. The parents buy a new radio and gramophone in their honour and immediately they try out an American record on which a singer called Ralph Wilton performs. While the record plays, the young newlyweds listen to the singer in the lounge taking them back to hearing her in the ship's lounge. The woman who is a big American patriot and who had earlier taken her leave at the American freedom tower, from the shining stars, from her free country, the man reminds her that <u>there is also freedom in Hungary</u>. Enough to know that Ralph Wilton fell in love with the woman and while the husband lies down, he vows love to the wife and urges her not to remain in Hungary, but she should return to America with him after meeting in Hamburg. He kisses the girl and after this, the girl (a Hungarian speaking American girl) behaves strangely, because Ralph Wilton spoke strongly against the trip to Hungary. Finally they arrive in Hamburg and from there, the newlyweds travel alone to Hungary. At home, the girl likes it very much and after an adventure, she reveals the Ralph Wilton affair to her husband and though the husband at first says that a Hungarian must keep his promise, if the wife says that she is not expecting a baby, then he will let her off. It was very nice and I would have liked it if you could have listened to it with me. The interval, instead of piano music they played the first few notes of the Rákóczi.

Perhaps now after this feeling of sensitivity, it is now time to return to reality and discuss our plans for the week.

Unfortunately I cannot come to London because it costs 14/8, of which the Government only gives 6/9 (which means going by coach) and sending things by train is so expensive, that I went to Crooks, (the transporters on whose lorry we came to London last time) and he will certainly do it more cheaply. Until then send me money to get my laundry and enough for the total travel costs to be paid. In the meanwhile I hope to get my results, but it makes no difference, because they will send it on to me.

I think that I have written everything, so I send a million kisses to all of you.

Andrew

P.S. Sorry that I am writing in pencil, but my ink has all been used up.

2

Alone in Melksham

Dearest Mum & Dad,

Thank you very much for yesterday's letter & contents, which I shall find very useful.

This time I have some very good news for you. The Cambridge results have arrived & they are even better than I expected.

I passed with distinction in

Mathematics

French

Shorthand

I passed with credit in

English language

English literature

History

Book-keeping

I failed in

Art

Thus with three distinctions & four credits I am exempt from taking Matriculation so long as I pay the fee. The failure in Art does not matter because it is my spare subject.

I am afraid I shall not come home till Sunday, because Saturday's bus is full up. I shall arrive at Victoria at the usual time i.e. 4.25 p.m. if I remember right. I am sending the bulk of my luggage by Crooks, the rest I shall carry. The bicycle will go by Crook's too. We can give the driver a tip when we meet the lorry at Olympia.

There is very little else to say. Mr. Redfearn will give me a nice testimonial, but you will see that yourselves. I shall leave about 1/- for John before I go, I cannot spare more. I shall not write any more now, & I am posting this right now so that you can get the results soon.

Lots of love from
Andrew

Moving On

This final letter from Andrew in Melksham marks his return to London, to pursue a career along lines discussed in his letters. I was now left in Melksham alone – for what was an unknown duration. My letters are more sporadic than Andrew's were, misspelled and much less erudite, if, perhaps, laced with more humour.

Notes from Father

The business began to do well and I was holding my breath waiting to see if I would get the job with the BBC. Early in 1941, Andrew came home from Melksham for good. He matriculated at 16, and a friend, an elderly stockbroker, got him a job in a firm of stockbrokers. He was paid around 30 shillings a week and proud to be a wage earner. He was first in his class at matriculation and his teachers gave him an exceptionally good letter of recommendation. Poor Johnny had to stay in Melksham alone.

Andrew was a big, tall and lanky boy, modest and sensible. He was very active with the Scouts, where they liked him and he became a Patrol Leader. He joined the group of firewatchers in the apartment block and he had to go to the roof of the house twice a week. Sometimes it was impossible to get home at night because the air raid was so heavy. Those times, we slept in the Pop Inn. Sometimes English friends came in for dinner and played bridge because they could not go out either. One night a tremendous explosion shook us all. The house opposite the Pop Inn was hit, the windows in the Pop Inn were broken and one of the counters fell over. We worked till the morning to get some semblance of order, so as not to have to close the restaurant. Next morning we heard that the owner of the restaurant opposite us, had gone home with his wife, thinking they would be safer there. Indeed, the windows of his restaurant were broken, but the house where they lived got a direct hit and they were dragged out of the rubble dead. My sweetheart wife, your Mum, how often she said that she would be very frightened if I were not at her side, but when we were together, she knew no fear.

John's original letter of 3 February 1941.
(Author's collection)

24 January 1941

Dear Mum & Dad,

I hope Andrew has arrived safely I am very sorry I could not see Andrew off. I got his hat and gas-mask but by the time I got back Andrew was gone with the wind. I will send it back as soon as I can. How are air-raids? I hope everything is O.K.

I am not getting on too badly and I hope I will soon get used to being alone. Have you heard from the B.B.C.

I am very proud that Andrew has passed the Cambridge so magnificently it was a wonderful effort, and I shouldn't be surprised the by the time he gets a firm of his own, he will earn about 10 pounds a week. I am sending the 'Hotspur' for Andrew. I could not get 'The Scout on Saterday' so I de-ordered it. Please write and send me some money and as soon as possible.

Lots of love from
John

P.S. Dear Sir (Mr. Oscar Forbat[23])

You were a silly twerp to forget your hat and gas-mask but I'll send it as soon as I get some money.

John

3 February 1941

Dear Mum and Dad,

I took my shoes (the ones Helen bought last year) down to the cobblers to have them mended, and they said that it can't be mended. So now I've only got one pair and I am shure that they wont last long as I had then at Christmas 1939 and the leather at the sides is getting very thin. So will you send me a pair as soon as you can. I take size fives. Please send me some money too please as I am nearly broke.

I am sending Andrew the 'Hotspur' and 'Champion' and 'Adventure'.

How are your getting on with the air-raids? I am getting on quite well. How is Noni and the rest of the family? Write soon.

John

Dear Oscar,

I just saw Dev Hills today and he asked me to remind you to write to him.

I am sending your three boocks so you should be satisfied.

Love from John.

P.S. My pills are getting low.

6 February 1941

Dear Mum and Dad,

I got your letter with the 2/6 on Tuesday, thank you very much. Have you got the gas-mask and hat? I sent them as soon as I got your letter. Please send me some shoes as soon as you can as I have no change. I need a jacket for school, as this one broadly speaking is almost in rags. Andrew can tell you that.

I am going to Trowbridge & the pictures tonight with Dev Hills.

My watch will be ready next Thursday wich will cost 4/- to 4/6, and I will have only a few coppers left when I come home from the pictures.

Please don't be angry that I am wanting a lot but I just can't help it.

Has Andrew got a job yet? And have you heard from the B.B.C.? I hope our are all well and the air-raids are light. Give Noni my love and 1,000,000 kisses. I hope to see you soon.

Lots of love and kisses from
John

P.S. Send Dev Hills his 1/-.

12 February 1941

Dear Mum & Dad,

I am sorry that I am so late in writing, I was going to write yesterday but I forgot.

I received your letter on Saturday and I am very glad to hear that Andrew has already got a job. I told Nick Redfearn[24] about Andrews job and he expected you to get a better job than that but it is only for a start. I told Mr. Marty[25] too and he is sending his kindest regards and congratulations. I could not tell Charlie[26] yet as he is not at school. Have you heard from the B.B.C.? Easter is coming soon and I hope I can go home for the holydays. Andrew wants me to imagine him as a fire-watcher, it is impossible. My watch is due to be ready to-morrow and I an nearly broke please send me some money

To day we had a history test and I got 25/25 full marks.

I hope you are all very well and raids are OK

How is Noni tell her I am sending her my love, and that I want to hear from her. Exams are coming soon (wish me luck). Please send me some more money as I only have a few coppers left I am quite well and have got used to being alone as I am usually with Les Fribbins my pal. I hope you will soon be able to send me a pair of shoes and a jacket. Write soon and send me some money soon please.

Millions of kisses and love from your loving son
John

10 March 1941

Dear Everybody,

How are you all getting on? I am very well. But I don't hear enough from you. Although you didn't send any mony last time I was lucky as I found 6*d* tucked away in my purse and Miss Ruby Hainz (Andrew can tell you who she is) gave me 6*d* on Sunday but I have 1/1 left, and 7*d* is being owed to me.

I am sending 'Hotspur' 'Champion' & 'Adventure' I haven't got that 'Adventure' that I borrowed yet, so you will have to read backwards.

I hope you will be able to send me some money and a parcle containing shirts, shoes if possible jacket socks, and my paint, and some chocolat if you can get it as we can't get it here. soon.

From now on when I get some money I'll put what I've got left from last time in the savings. How is Andrews job? I want to know all about it. Have you heard from the B.B.C.?

Easter Monday is on April 14. so I hope to be home with you all soon. On Wednesday I am taking a trade scolalrship which might get me to a secondary school if I am lucky.

I heard the London had some bad raids throughout the week end I hope everything is OK. Is the Pop Inn getting on well? How is Noni? And I want to know if the kitten is any better. I want you to write more at least twice a week. I do, so why shouldn't you?

Do you have many raids? We had a few warnings lately but nothing happens.

You'll have to congratulate Melksham as they are building 3 surface shelters. I still have not been able to read the 'Adventure' that I missed so try and send it to get it.

For our History exams we have got to learn about 2 or 3 dozen dates (only ahem) and write out facts about 10 people in history. If Andrew was here I'd disguise him as myself and let him take my place but I am unlucky. But I'm not worrying much about history much. Geography is the one I am worreing about. I'll have to finish now as I have to swot up those History dates yet. So I'll have to finish off.

9999 millions x1009 kisses from your loving John

22 April 1941

Dear Darlings,

I have not been able to get Andrew's gas-mask yesterday but I got it at dinner-time after school to-day. Mrs. Robbins has not yet given me the money for the eggs in fact she has not even mentioned anything about giving me it. I arrived at Melksham fairly early and I saw a procession for the War wepons week. And in some of the big shops windows are parachutes lewis-guns, tommy guns rubber dhingies, camara guns and camaras that are fitted to reconnasence planes, and the town is full of posters which the boys & girls have have done and flags. I have not seen my poster yet.

Has daddy got to Evesham safely? I have bought an other 6*d* savings stamp and I have 7/- in the savings now. We have had very good wether and it is nice and hot. Have you got my report yet. I am sending the gas mask and the 'Adventure'. How is everybody please write soon. Daddy has not written to me yet.

92345678901267 3/100 3/100 millions of kisses from your everloving
John

Notes from Father

Slowly spring arrived. In the middle of April, there was a prediction in the astrology column of the Sunday Express *that a long-awaited event would happen. I thought, that could only mean the BBC. The following morning the telephone rang. They called from the BBC that I should go to the Establishment Officer at once in connection with my job, because it was now open. We could barely wait with excitement for the next day. When I went, they received me saying that for the summer vacations, about seven months, they could employ me, but I would have to go to Evesham, because that was where the work was done. They warned me that the job was only till the autumn, and I should accept it only if it does not mean giving up something more certain. My pay would be £7 (rather than the £2/10/- at the Pop Inn) and they would pay for lodging and simple daily meals. The work would be for five days a week, two days free when I would be free to go to London, once a month at the expense of the BBC. The work schedule would be 8 a.m. to 4 p.m. one week, 4 p.m. to midnight the next and from midnight to 8 a.m. the third. Without thinking, I accepted the job, hoping that after the holiday period they might retain me. Although it was painful that we would not be together for five days a week, we were happy that there was such a great improvement in my earning capacity. Instead of being the manager of a small restaurant, I received a serious, responsible position, which would help in some way in the war effort. As an alien, I had been under certain restrictions. I had to be off the streets by midnight and was not allowed to have a radio, etc. As an important government employee, these restrictions were lifted.*

I travelled to Evesham, 2 hours from London; I was both happy and sad. I was met by a woman, the billeting officer, at the railway station, who showed me where I was to stay. There were two others who were hired on the same terms as I was. My flat was a horror. It was a nice little house, with a room in the attic. It had no window, only a vent, which let the rain in when opened. The furniture consisted of a horrible small bed, an ugly cupboard and a washstand. The owner of the house was a young widow, who herself had to go to work, so she did not provide breakfast as in other billets. A bus took me to work, half an hour from Evesham, in a beautiful park where there were barracks. I was allocated in one of these, in Unit Y. I began work at 4 p.m. The place was filled all kinds of radios, connections and recorders with which we used to record what we heard on to discs. On the first day it looked too complicated and I was afraid I would not be able to learn to use it. One radio could receive five or six stations and one had to pay attention every moment to see what was happening at the various German broadcasts and everything had to be written down on paper. My English was far from perfect, my spelling was not good and I could not see well in the lighting there. I wrote to Mum to send me a Hungarian–English dictionary and my glasses, which I had not been using at that time. They introduced me to the supervisor, who struck me as being a very big man, and to the chief, a young Englishman called Shankland, who seemed a very important person in my eyes. I was very impressed with the other monitors who knew their work so well. I was worried how I would learn all this. There were monitors from all kinds of nationalities in Evesham but our unit only had Germans, Austrians and one Hungarian besides me. Every two hours during the work, we were allowed to go to the canteen for tea and later for dinner. It was always arranged that while one was in the canteen, another colleague would be listening to the broadcasts.

I wrote to Mum almost every day and kept counting the days before I could come and see her in London. On her advice, I did not come home every third week, because the time would have been very short. I finished work at midnight and two days later I had to start at 8 a.m., and as I could not travel till the morning, I would not have had to return the following afternoon. Nevertheless, sometimes I used even that short period, because I longed for her terribly. Every third week I was able to stay in London for three days, because I finished work at 4 p.m. and after two days' leave, I did not start work till midnight, so I got to return to Evesham in the afternoon of the third day.

I got to learn the work fairly quickly and I got used to it. The supervisors liked me and I had friendly relationship with my colleagues, although I did not develop a close relationship with any of them. I did not spend much time in the billet, because it was uncomfortable and unfriendly. I asked them to place me in a better one. The food in the canteen was not too enjoyable. Because of the war, hardly anything good was available. If we got an egg, it was counted like a feast day. It was hard to get cigarettes; I always brought some from London.

Johnny was not too far from me in Melksham and I brought him over for two or three days when he was on holiday. We were both happy. He slept with me in my narrow bed, we could hardly turn, but we both felt comfortable. When I went to work till 4 p.m., he slept part of the time and looked round the town part of the time. He was 12, and in my eyes still a little boy and it worried me that he was on his own. He had to go to have his breakfast alone, I gave him money and told him where to go. I sent him to the club for lunch and asked the waitress to take care of him and after I returned, we had a happy afternoon and evening together. When he had to return next day, I could not be with him when he got on the bus, because I had to leave the house at 7 a.m. and forgetting how independent I had been when I was 12, I worried whether he got on the right bus or that no trouble should come his way. He promised to send me a card as soon as he arrived and a big stone fell from my heart when I received his card that all was well.

At the same time, I awaited Mum's letters and counted the days before I came home. How happy these homecomings were? Mum was more and more occupied in the Pop Inn; Uncle Eugene put her behind the counter as 'bar manageress', she served drinks and got tips, which I could not bear, but she insisted that this would improve your income, which had now increased to £3. For this reason, she became the pillar of the business. She opened it at 8 a.m. and closed it at midnight. She took care of the stores, which was a very tiring job and her feet began to ache from standing all day. She had one day off and two hours in the afternoon. That was taken up with going home, having a bath and returning, so there was not much opportunity for rest. Nevertheless she wrote a sweet letter to me every night before going to bed, so that in the five days when I was away from her, I was not without news. When I was in London, I sat by the bar and watched how she served the people. Despite her work, everyone treated her as a lady. They knew that she was the proprietor's sister-in-law, and her appearance and behaviour elicited everyone's respect.

One beautiful spring morning when I got home after five nights of work, as I arrived in London, to my joy she was awaiting me at the train station, together with Andrew. As always, she had a sweet dress and Andrew with a beautiful new suit, which he bought from his own earnings. You were both extremely proud that our son could buy clothes out of his own money, only I was not happy that the poor boy had to work and that I was not buying it for him. I did not know about it beforehand, it was a big surprise. Only our Johnny was missing. The three days at home was like a new honeymoon, actually all my homecomings counted as such. Unfortunately Mum had to work during the time and her feet hurt even more from much standing.

The days in Evesham were much of the same thing. When I had night work, I got to bed about 10 in the morning, but I had trouble getting used to sleeping during the day. I spent a lot of time with a friendly family and made friends with a few colleagues, women, girls and men who were my fellow workers. I tried to be very conscientious in my work. On one occasion I noticed that a German station broadcast music for a whole hour, and the composer of each piece began with the letter M. I reported this, and the chief called me to his office, praised me that my attention had included this, and said I should notice these things again. A few days later, a colleague asked me what I had discovered for the chief to praise me (he sat next to me at work) and I told him. A few weeks later, the chief called us all into the office and said that some people had talked about their work and everyone should know that this is strictly forbidden. Sometimes I felt that he was referring to my indiscretion although he gave no sign of this. It seemed as though this was about some different serious matter, although previously I had not even thought that I had done anything wrong. Everyone in the hut knew that I had made some sort of 'discovery' and everyone had listened to the German broadcasts, yet my conscience was not clear. To this day I do not know whether he directed his remarks at me or to someone else.

Soon Mum was due for a few days' holiday and we were happily planning that she would spend it with me in Evesham. I talked to the Beasleys, who readily agreed that she should stay in my room and they would give her, her meals. We could barely wait for the day when the day of her free time would arrive. I had a narrow bed in my room, but we thought that we would be able to get into it together. We arranged that Mum should come on a week when I was working from 8–4, so that the afternoon and evenings were ours. I waited for her with the excitement of waiting for a new bride until she arrived on August 1. I would have brought down the stars of the sky to make her stay with her happy and it was successful. We had dinner in the club each night. While I was at work, she looked around the town on her own. She made an excursion to Stratford-on-Avon to see the Shakespeare memorabilia. In the afternoon, she was waiting for me at the bus station as I came back from work. We only had one problem. My bed was too narrow for both of us and we were afraid that if one of us were to turn, the other would fall out. We did not mind this discomfort. When I got up at 6 a.m., Mum was able to stretch out and sleep comfortably for a few hours.

Our only worry was that the 'holiday relief' season was coming to an end and there were no indications that I would be retained in the job. I had a day off on my birthday, August 7, and I could not bear the uncertainty. We got on a bus and went to see the chief and asked for an interview. I was at least able to show Mum my workplace. She waited on a bench while I was with the chief. I asked about my prospects and he said, definitely none. My employment would be over in the middle of October. I was very distressed and she knew the result of the interview by looking at my face. As I knew that one of three temporary workers was retained, the matter hurt me even more.

24 *April 1941*

Dear Dad,

I got our card this dinner time and I was pleased to hear from you. I inquired about the bus to Evesham and I was told that I should have to go to Bath on the Bath bus and go by some other service from there. And I don't know what service to go by. So If I wand to go by bus I shall have to go to Bath I shall have to go to Bath beforehand and make enquiries etc. So I went down to the G.W.R. station and asked about the trains and there they told me that I could get a train on Friday at 4.6 p.m. and the fares would be 10/3 return which is very dear so I am at a loss what to do as I want to come. And even then I'll not be able to come till next week as you don't get your pay until Saturday.

John

25 *April 1941*

Dear Dad,

The fares which I wrote yesterday were wrong instead of it being 10/3 it is 7/11 ½ by train to Evesham so it will not be so bad. Please write and tell me what week-end to come and send the money. Please send soon pocket money too. As I have but ½d left and Mrs. Robbins has not even suggested paying me for the Easter eggs. Lots of love and kisses

John

28 April 1941

Dear Mum and Andrew,

Thank you very much for the socks and the belt. They are very nice. I am very sorry to say that I have again lost my fountain pen and this time I have not got it back. I had a letter from daddy today and he says that he is going to London for Friday & Saturday. And I am very pleased too that I most likely to be able to go to Evesham and see him, the week after he goes to see you , as he is off Saturday and Sunday. On Saturday (this week) I am going to Bath to enquire which bus service I have to use, and perhaps book my seat. I am sending the 'Hotspur' 'Champion' & 'Adventure'. I am not expecting the money back from Mrs. Robbins as I think she is taking it for granted that the Easter eggs were a present (I don't blame her). How are you? How is Andrew and Noni? (Write soon please I will write to daddy when he sends some money as I am broke all but 1*d*. He said he is sending some Tuesday which will get here on Wednesday.

I have nothing else to write so good bye $9264x^2 - 2yz$ millions of kisses from your ever-loving John.

2 May 1941

Dear Everybody,

I am sending the report in this letter. The school is paying 1*d* for the stamp and I have to pay the 1½*d*. I am quite broke and I had to lend the money for the letter. Daddy wrote in his last letter that he is sending some money Tuesday which should have got here Wednesday but I have not heard from him at all yet. How is everybody? At the moment it is bad weather hear. It has been raining all the morning. Please write soon. How is Noni and Andrew? Is he still at his job? I hope I'll get some money to night from dad as I want to go to Bath tomorrow to make enquiries.

Love & kisses from
John

P.S. I am sorry I have been so long sending this letter as I expected to get the report on Friday but I could not get it till Monday. I went to Bath on Saturday and I booked my seats to Evesham for next week-end to see daddy. Lots of love & kisses from your ever-loving

John

2 May 1941

Dear Everyone,

I am terribly sorry that I forgot to mention about Daddy's photo which you sent me. I was ever-so pleased with it and I think it is a very good picture. Please (if possible) send one of Mummy and Andrew too.

I am very glad that at last you agree with me and let me wear my new suit. I am sure I'll look more like a human being. I promise I'll take care of it as much as possible.

By the way please send me at least two pairs of socks immediately (if possible) for as you know these are in pieces.

I went to Trowridge pictures to-day and again got in for 16. The pictures were very good. One was Laurel & Hardy one called 'Great Guns' and the other one was called 'Man at large' which was also very good and had two or three murders in it (that's all) hm hm!!

I have got an allotment free from the school & I share it with Jim Gurr, we have already dug it up and have planted some seeds, then when they come up I can sell the food and make a profit.

I am looking forward to seeing you all soon and I shouldn't be surprised if in 3 weeks time we should all be together. Has Dad heard from the B.B.C. yet? Give my love to Noni, and I hop[e] Andy has swatted many flies.

Lots of love and kisses from your everloving
John

3 May 1941

Dear Dad,

I am at Bath and I have made the necessary enqueries about the bus. It is 4/- return. I leave Bath at 11.50 change at Cheltenham at 2.40.

So I am now going to get out of the savings 4/- and book the seats. Please wait for me at the bus (on Saturday).

Lots of love & kisses from
John

15 May 1941

Dear Daddy,

I arrived safely in Melksham at 6 o' clock after having to wait for the bus from Bath till about 5.15. We have started to learn shorthand & bookkeeping. How are you getting on? Have you heard from Mummy yet? I am writing to her to-day and I shall try to persuade her to learn ride a bicycle

I hop[e] to see you soon.

Lots of love & kisses from
John

5 June 1941

Dear Daddy,

I got your letter from London with the money in it. Thank you very much for the 2/6. I got your letter from Evesham to day too and I thought you would already have known that I've got the measles as I wrote to London about it while you were there. Anyway I will not be able to go home for Witsun week as I must not get in a crowd for 3 weeks. All my spots have gone and I most likely getting up (out of bed) tomorrow. If I do go home I shall have to go when the 3 weeks are over which will mean another week away from school. But I should like to go home very much. So do your best. Has Mummy passed the B.B.C. test in Italian?

I think she ought to take German [test] as well. Write and tell me if I will be able to go home after my measles are gone.

How are you getting on? By the way I want to go home too because I am supposed to get a new suit.

Lots of love and millions of kisses from your everloving John

P.S. My writing is so bad because I am in bed.

6 June 1941

Dear Daddy,

I got your letter this morning and I am pleased that you have got a new and better billet.

I got a letter from mummy on Monday and she said that Tiggy has got another three kittens. I hope she keeps the nicest one. Please do not worry about my illness. I am not in bed any more and all my spots are gone. Only the three weeks quarenteen keep me from school. I will be going to London next Wednesday or Thursday. I shall know for shure on Monday. I have already been outside.

I am not shure wether you live at 10 or 19 Broadway Road please write it clearly. I hope mummy passed the exam although I am shure she will. I think she ought to try German as well as Italian. How are you getting on? I am quite well but I am lonely as I must not go near anyone so I can't go out to do anything

Lots of love and kisses from your everloving
John

24 June 1941

Dear Daddy,

I arrived in Melksham safely on Sunday and after tea I went swimming. I got my new suit this morning and it fits very well.

I hope you are getting on alright with your work. I am very well.

The weather is very nice and I am going swimming again to-day. Please write soon.

I am a bit behind at school but I will soon catch up.

I have learned to swim under water with my eyes open and swim between anybody's legs (under water) And to tuch the bottom with my hands in the 9 foot 6 ins.

I don't know when we are breaking up for summer but let us hope it will soon come. I have no more news so I'll send lots of love and millions of kisses from your everloving.

John

27 June 1941

Dear Dad,

I got your letter this morning and I am answering strait away so that you will have time t[o] send the money. I am very willing to come to Evesham and if you think it is more worth for me to go to Evesham than for you to go to London, then send the money and I will book my seets. I am quickly catching up in school. It was rather hard for me to read your card this morning as the silly fools at the post office put the stamp mark right in the middle of your writing. On Sunday Mrs. Robbins is taking me to Weston Super Mare for the day where we can swim in the sea. Yesterday it was 5 years that we came to England.

I hope you are getting on all right I am very well. I got my suit on Tuestay and it fits very well and it is very nice. I hope to see you on the 5th Saturday. How is your work. I took my shoes to be nailed but they said is must be soled so will you please send money for that too (3/9) as soon as you can.

Lots of love and kisses from your everloving
Johnnie

3 July 1941

Dear Dad,

I got your letter and money yesterday and I wrote to Bath for a ticket and sent them the 4/-. They should have got that to-day so I hope to get the ticket by Friday.

I am afraid that this time I shall have to come back on Sunday as I have missed 3 weeks of school and the teacher will only be full of sarcasm if I am not at school. Why didn't you send me some money to get my shoes done? Unless I can get them out without paying straight away I shall have to come in my plimsoles which Mrs. Robbins gave me.

How are you getting on? I can hardly wait to see you. I hope you are getting on well in your job.

I had my new suit on Sunday and I looked very smart in it. I have no other news.

$964240x^5$ kisses and lots of love from your everloving
John

P.S. I am coming Saturday 2.40 as usual.

4 July 1941

Dear Dad,

I am very sorry to say that I will not be able to come to Evesham as you did not send the money soon enough. I got a letter from Bath in which they had sent back the 4/- postal order and said that all the seets had been booked up. I should have booked up at least 3 days beforehand. I[f] you had sent the money earlier it would have been O.K. as I got the money on Wednesday which allows them to get it on Thursday which is too late.

It is a great dissappointment as I was looking forward to seing you with all my heart.

But I hope to see you soon. I will spend the 4/- on getting my shoes done. Please write and send some money for next week.

Have you had any air raids?

I have no more news.

Lots of love & kisses from your everloving
John

10 July 1941

Dear Daddy,

I got your letter on Tuesday and I was even more dissappointed that I couldn't go to Evesham when I heard that Andrew was there. Thank you very much for the 3/-. I have bought a 6*d* savings stamp. I go swimming and I can dive head first ads jump off the top board. How are you getting on? I am fine and I hope to see you soon. We are breaking up for summer on the 15th of August.

Did you go swimming with Andrew? The wether is lovely & hot and I am going swimming again to-day. I have no more news. Please write soon. I hope you will enjoy yourself in London.

Lots of love and kisses from your everloving
John

17 July 1941

Dearest Dad,

I gladly received your letter this afternoon after a long expectant week, as I have not had a letter from you for over a week. You wanted to know how school is. On Wednesday we had a little test of shorthand and I came top with full marks. I was inoculated to day by the school against diphtheria. Thank you for the money.

I know now for sure that we are breaking up for the summer holydays on the 15th of August to return on the 8th of September (3 weeks). Please send the money for the fares to go home as soon as possible so that I can book up and make sure of getting a seat.

I have not been swimming lately as the weather has not been so good. I am very well and I hope you are. I will most likely get another 6d savings samp as I have only 2/6 in the saving. I hope to see you in just over 4 weeks time.

Lots of love and kisses from your everloving
John

25 July 1941

Dear Dad,

I got your letter 26 minutes ago and I am glad to hear that Mum will be at Evesham and that I can see you and go home to London with Mum. Thank you very much for the 2/6.

I hope you will not be angry that I tore my new trousers. But I have been punished as I had to take money out of the savings to have it mended. It cost 1/- and it is done so well that you can hardly see it was torn.

I am very glad that I shall see you in less than 3 weeks time and I can hardly wait. I shall have to come on Thursday 14th August as Mum will most likely leave Evesham in the morning. I might have to come by train because they are stopping the busses I shall enquire and tell you details next time I write.

I hope you are all well. I have now news.

Lots of love and kisses from your everloving John

P.S. Please send fares in good time as I want to make sure of a seat.

Dear Mum and Dad,

I went to Weston Super Mare on Friday with Mrs. Robbins and had a lovely time on the beach. We got there about 11.45 a.m. we stayed on the beach till dinner and for another two hours. Then we went on the pier where there was a fair I went on the dodgems and the were some machines where you have to put a penny in and have to fire a gun at a number of small objects. If you hit them all down you get your penny back I got mine back twice out of about eight goes. And I had a go at the moter boat dodgems. We got back home at about 9.50 p.m.

Please send me at least three pairs of socks as mine are very thin and get holes in them very easily. Please write more often for if you do not we may get worried because of the many air raids. How are you all getting on? I hope Noni is getting used to the air raids.

Congratulations to dad for the exam.

Lots of love for all *from John*

4 August 1941

Dear Dad,

I got your letter this morning after an expectant wait for over a week please wrote more frequently.

Thank you very much for the 2/6. I don't think the busses are not running any more to Evesham as they are not running to London or any long distances. So I'll have to go by train the fair (half single) I believe is 7/9½. Please send the fares as soon as possible so that I can book up. I can hardly wait for the 10 days to go untill I see you.

We have got a holiday to-day. I have no more new. I am very well and I hope you are too. I hope you will enjoy being with Mummy.

Lots of love from your everloving
John

4 August 1941

Dear Mum & Andrew,

I am sorry I am so late in writing but I didn't have any money till this morning when I got a letter from dad after a long wait of over a week. I can hardly wait till the 10 days are over when I shall see you. I am sending Andrew 'Hotspur' & 'Champion'. I hope Andrew will write more. We have a holyday to day as it is bank holyday. I hope you will enjoy yourself at Evesham. I don't think the busses are running to Evesham as there are no busses running to London or any long distances so I'll have to go by train the fare of which is 7/9½ (half single). On Thursday the king and Queen came through Melksham and I saw them both. I hope you are all well. How is Noni. I am very well. There is no more news here so lots of

Love & kisses from your everloving
John

11 *August 1941*

Dear Mum & Dad,

Last Friday not beins sure wether the busses are running to Evesham or not I borrowed 4/- from Mrs. Robbins and sent for a ticket at Bath. But when I received a ticket from you on Saturday I was in a bit of a mess so to-day when received the letter from Bathe with a ticket I sent it back and asked for the money back. So I hope it will be all right. I hope you got my birthday-card. I wish daddy the best of luck and good health for life which I wish to be a lengthy one.

I am dying to see you but Thursday will come soon. I hope you are enjoying yourself together. I have no more news.

Lots of & kisses from your everloving
John

P.S. I can only put 1*d* on the envelope as that is all the money I have.

8 *September 1941*

Dear Mum,

I arrived safely yesterday and when I went to bed I felt as if I was lying on a brick wall after being used to your bed. I hope you are not feeling too lonely. I cannot write to dad to-day as I have not enough paper. There is a fair here and I am going there as soon as I have finished this letter.

When I told the boys that you wont let me swim in the deep part of the river they were surprised and rightfully laughed. Thad is further proof that it is not dangerous. I hope you will realise this and give me permission.

Please send my things after me soon as possible. I have no more news so I will say good-bye. Please write soon.

Lots of love from John

10 September 1941 – partly written in Pitman shorthand

Dear Dad & Andrew,

I arrived safely in Melksham on Monday and I was very sad to leave Mum alone.

Today I had my second inoculation. I hope you are enjoying yourselves.

I am sending the 'Adventure'. Please send some money. Have you had any news from the 'big shots' of the B.B.C. wether they will keep you or not. There is no news here. I wrote to Mum on Monday. I hope to see you soon.

Will Andrew try to read the following:- [See the image below.]

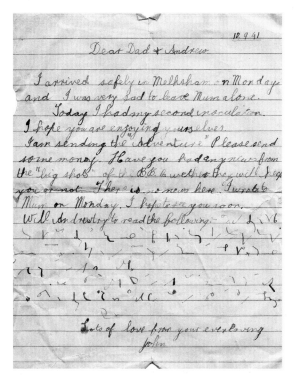

John showing off his Pitman shorthand. (Author's collection)

Notes from Father

At that time the war was going on with full force in Russia. The Germans occupied Russia, apparently without resistance and the news was bad everywhere. I was optimistic concerning a final victory, but not optimistic about getting another job, and most importantly, maintain Mum in a relatively free existence, to free her from her heavy work. As always, she consoled and encouraged me, but it was the end of our time of happiness and her days off.

Andrew had a few days' leave and he came down to see me in Evesham. He too slept in my bed; somehow we were able to get in together. He also awaited me with his bicycle at the bus station. He was 16 years old, a tall and lanky young man. I went to the club with him, played ping-pong and darts with him and he tried to teach me to ride a bicycle. That was unsuccessful; I sat on the bike on one side and fell off the other. In the BBC orchestra there was a very nice man, who had the reputation of being able to play the violin beautifully. I used to play ping-pong with him; when he made a mistake, he slapped his own face. I asked him to hear Andrew play, whether it was worth while his taking lessons again. We went to his flat, where he allowed Andrew to play the Minuet in G by Beethoven on his 'cheap' violin, and then he took his 'expensive' violin and played it on that. Andrew and I were both moved as we listened to a great artist. At my request, he then played Kreisler's Rosemarie. He played so beautifully, that I had tears in my eyes. Later, I invited the young German lady who had an English husband, to the Crown Hotel, one of the best in Evesham, for lunch, together with Andrew. Somehow our friendship began. Andrew's holiday ended a few days later and I was left alone once again. I was very depressed, without confidence in the future or looking for another position. I had a little money in the bank but that would only last a few weeks. Mum wrote me that as I would not be staying much longer, I should save money and not come home every week (or rather, twice every three weeks), but only once in three weeks. This hurt me a lot, but I knew that she missed me too.

When I came home once more, our relationship was a little more commonplace than it used to be. Mum was also tired from her work and worry concerning my future. I returned to Evesham for the last time.

16 September 1941

Dear Dad,

I am happy to know that Andrew enjoyed himself with you and it is a pity that I forgot to tell you that Mr. Robbins was in Evesham as you could have looked him up. I hope you are not feeling very lonely. I have settled myself at Melksham but I AM LONGING TO SEE YOU.

There is not much news here in Melksham. Please write soon and send some money. Last week Eugene bácsi [Uncle Eugene] sent my 2/6 to spend at the fair which was at Melksham.

Please write soon as I am always happy when I get a letter from you.

Lots of love & kisses from your everloving
John

P.S. I went to pictures last night & Mrs. Robbins treated me.

23 September 1941

Dear Dad,

I want to wish you a happy Roshashono. I didn't go to school yesterday and to-day, and I went to Broughton Gifford where the[re] was a service. I will go on Jankipur too.

Exams will start in less than 2 weeks time and I hope I will be rather high up.

Please send some money as you didn't send any last week. I miss you very much and I am longing to see you. There is no new here so I'll finish.

Lots of love and kisses from your everloving
John

28 September 1941

Dear Dad,

I was very pleased to get your letter last week & thank you very much for the 2/6. I am very sorry that you will have to leave the B.B.C. but still something may turn up. I am glad to hear that Andrew in now at the Chelsea Polytechnic day course. We Started our exams last week and I hope to be nearer the top than last time. I hope you are feeling well. I am but I miss you every so. I heard that we are having a weeks holyday at the end of October, can I come home?

Please write soon. I have no more news.

Wishing you a good Jankipur from your everloving John

18 October 1941

Dear Everybody,

I got your letter yesterday and I was very happy to know that Daddy has hopes of going back to the B.B.C. I am also glad that you got the blackburies. We are breaking up for our holyday on Friday 24th so I will be able to come home on the Saturday morning. Tom is treating me to the pictures to-night, and yesterday he bought me a lovely 3/6 aeroplane book. I might bring another lot of blackburies with me when I come home. I am glad Andrew is happy at school. I hope you are all O.K. Give Noni my love. I will bring home my torch and aeroplane with me so that you will be able to see them. I have joined the school library and I've got a very good book. I am glad you have stopped worrying about Tom.[27] Thanks a lot for the 2/6.

We have had 5 of our exam results:-
Arithmetic 65. Art 64. Book-keeping 50. Maths 55. Science 70. my average up to now being 60.8 but when I get my shorthand marks (which might be 75) it will I hope) rise.

I have no more news.

Lots of love & kisses from you everloving John

Please Send Money

The occasional letter I wrote to my impecunious parents had the same two themes: 'please send money' and, 'why can't I have long trousers like all the other boys in my class?' Often, I didn't have the money for a stamp and found that rubbing the corner of the envelope made it look like the stamp had fallen off. Clothing coupons adding to food ration books limited the nation's consumption and though my letter always arrived, never my long trousers and rarely a shilling. I seemed to be the only boy without a bicycle, but my first paper round for W.H. Smith seriously began to enrich me, involving a mile or two's walk before breakfast and school.

A horny teenager, the big bag of newspapers I had to lug around served well to hide the projection in the front of my shorts as I delivered my newspapers around the town. When I was promoted to 'putting up' the rounds for the other boys, initially from a book showing each customer's mix of papers and magazines and later having learned it by heart, my raise to 5/- a week was like falling into Aladdin's cave. However, with my much earlier 6 o' clock start, I overslept a couple of times and was warned I would go back on the round if I were late one more time. Waking up to light in the window next morning, I had dressed and wolfed down a sneaked slice of bread, before I saw the clock on the kitchen mantelpiece. I had woken at 2 a.m. to a full moon!

With all that money, I was able to buy a kit and build an elastic-powered, propeller-driven scale model Hawker Hurricane – an early modelling attempt with representative balsa wood structure and doped paper covering. It looked like the real thing and I could hardly wait to get it home to London at the start of the Christmas holiday. Jumping the gun of patience, I launched it in the railway station car park and after executing a graceful circle, it crashed ignominiously onto the hard tarmac breaking its meticulously carved propeller. A long face accompanied my creation to London and it never flew again.

Existing in the lowest ranks of the RAF on 1/- a day, 21-year-old AC2 Tommy G. Williams from 'The Camp' outside town befriended me

Different boy, same bag. (Author's collection)

in the park when he found out that I was a Scout, as he had been. Like a good mentor, he helped to sort out the aftermath of my beating by the three thugs and we spent a lot of time discussing the world. He got me interested in Esperanto and our Con Kora Saluto salutation adorned each letter in our later correspondence. I had little idea as to why my parents were worried by a grown man's interest in their little son so far away, but meeting him seemed to relieve their fears. A devout Catholic, he subsequently entered the Church and we corresponded during his years as a missionary in India.

19 November 1941

Dear Mum, Dad & Andrew,

I was very pleased to get your letter on Monday after a wait of 1 week & 3 days. But all the same thanks for the 3/-. I can't see why you want me to write more seeing that I wrote twice before I got a letter from you.

I am glad you liked my poetry I hope you are all getting on all right. Has Andrew written to Mr. Borton yet? By the way, please write and answering letter to Tom.

I have still got 13 candles left from my last birthday, so if you can please try and send me a birthday-cake. Give my love to Noni and everybody. Time is flying to me and in a week I will be thirteen.

By the way am I getting a watch. I have now got 2/- in the savings. Tell Andrew that Mr. Williams & Mr. Parkin are leaving Melksham and are going back to London. Our class is collecting some money amongst ourselves to buy Mr. Williams a present and I gave 6d.

I have no more news so I'll close down

Lots of love & kisses from your everloving
John

3

Internment and Illness

6 December 1941

Dear Everybody,

I must wish Mum many happy returns on her birthday, and I hope she will be pleased with the tea-cosy which I sent her yesterday. I wish you, Mum, the best of luck health and happiness for the rest of your life which I hope will last till at least you are 126 3/19 years old. I am Okay and I am looking forward to seing you in 2 weeks. Tell Andrew I thank him very much for the line he dropped and tell him I hope he catches it. By the way how is his young lady getting on? Tell her that I thank her very much for the birthday greetings

I have no more news. I am going to pictures to-night with Tom.

Give my love to Noni and everyone else.

Lots of love & kisses from your everloving
John

9 December 1941

Dear Mum & Dad,

I was pleased to get your letter yesterday but please send some pocket money as I don't want to spend the remaining 4/-. Why I have only that left is because I have spent 6/- on presents.

I hope Mum is pleased with her tea-cosey. Please write at once a[s] I want to know if everything is O.Kay about the internment as I am worried. The shorthand that I am sending is for Andrew. I hope you are well and I am desperately looking forward to sing you, and Christmas will be here soon. By the way I'll need railway fares soon.

I have no more news so I'll close down.

Lots of love & kisses from your everloving John

Notes from Father

My little money kept diminishing. I could not find work and spent part of my time in the Pop Inn, watching Mum as she served the guests, and partly in the bridge club. Meanwhile, Andrew increasingly wanted to leave his work as a secretary in the Pop Inn in order to go to University. He wanted to become a doctor. We liked the idea, but I had no idea how I could take on such a responsibility in my financial position. I could not even afford his first school fee.

I tried everything, but could not find a job anywhere and I did not have the money to start any kind of business. The bombing had eased, but the Germans were conquering everywhere and the future did not look good. One morning, on Mum's birthday, December 7, 1941, we woke to the news that the Japanese, without any warning, had bombed a large portion of the American fleet in Pearl Harbor. As bad as this news was, everyone in England was relieved that at last America was involved in the war on our side, even against her will. Out of the German butchery of Jews, British, French and Poles, a world war had broken out. America declared war on Japan and Germany. In Italy, Mussolini felt that the time had come to join the Germans, since he had no doubt that Germany would win. The Germans forced Hungary into the war and suddenly we became enemy aliens. On Germany's orders, Hungary interned all the British there, and the British interned some of the Hungarians, even though most of them were refugees from Hungarian anti-Semitism. Feri Áldor [a friend] was among the first. He was considered an undesirable alien even in peacetime.

On December 8th they took Uncle Imre as well. Mum was terrified lest they would take me as well. Uncle Eugene was already a British subject and he was not in danger, and I was certain that I would not be interned, since there could be no doubt of my reliability, having been employed in a secret department of the BBC. But she was anxious and I could not calm her down. On the morning of December 13th, the doorbell rang at about 6 or 7 a.m. Mum sat up in bed and began to sob – this could only be police, 'I knew they were going to take you too,' she said. I went to the door and indeed there were two policemen outside. They asked if Andrew was at home.

I said, yes, he is asleep. Wake him, they said, we have instructions to take him to the internment camp. Mum was standing behind me at the door, completely upset. I said to the policeman, there must be some mistake; you must have come for me and not for my 16-year-old son. They replied, there is no mistake, he will be 17 in another two weeks and in any case, those are our instructions. Don't be afraid, he will not come to any harm. As much as this pained Mum, that her young son was being taken away, she was relieved that they did not take me. She said that a young lad can bear the discomforts associated with internment and she could bear it better if I were with her. The policemen were very nice, Mum quickly packed the essentials for Andrew, and soon we were all on the way down the corridor with our son. Our hearts ached but we decided that we would do everything possible to free him.

A Mistake

Between December 1941 and January 1942 Andrew was interned as an enemy alien with many others aliens, including an uncle, on the Isle of Man. He even spent his 17th birthday there, but was thankfully released after a few weeks. Neither of my parents was interned. After the war was over, the Home Office admitted that Andrew was interned by mistake.

12 December 1941

Dear Mum & Dad & Noni,

I am just dropping you a line to say that I am quite all right. I was in Chelsea all day yesterday together with 14 other Hungarians & we slept there. I am on the train now on way to a camp near Manchester. It might be some time before you hear again from me as letters will be censored. I shall write to say where I am & if you try to get a Home Office Permit, there is every possibility of you seeing me. I hope you are all right & Daddy is still at home. Please send me a towel as soon as you get my address. In future I shall be restricted to 20 lines twice a week, so that I can't write much. Don't forget that to inform the Polytechnic & if possible Mr. Young, 96 Lower Richmond Rd. Putney S.W.15.

Don't worry about me at all I am all right, food is plenty, beds O.K. Write you more from camp as I am doing this in secret. A nice soldier who escorted me promised to take it to you.

Hope to be out by the time John comes but is unlikely

Lots of love & hundreds of kisses from
Andrew

26 December 1941

From:- Andrew Forbat 95405, RM Camp IOM
OPENED BY EXAMINER 7106
Dear Mum, Dad, Noni & John,

At last I am able to write to you to say that I am quite all right &
there should be no cause for worry on your part. I spent my first day
in London, & slept there. Next morning we were taken to a camp in
Manchester. On Monday we came here to the Isle of Man. The food is
quite sufficient & good. Beds, treatment etc. all very satisfactory. Here all
the Hungarians are in one house, originally a hotel, & there are about 70
of us. I sleep in one room with Uncle Imre. The weather is surprisingly
like spring here, during the day we get quite warm sunshine. We go for
a nice walk every day amid glorious scenery. Generally I find plenty to
do in the house in helping to keep the house clean etc. Please send me
towel, collars, shirts, other suit, & laundry generally. One of you please
go to my locker B40 in the Polytechnic (porter will tell you how to find
it) & bring send me my biology & mechanics test-books if possible. I
hope to speak to the Int. Officer next time but I do not expect to be out
before February unless something exceptional turns up. Hope Daddy is
still at home?[29] I shall write again next week & do not worry if letters
take long to come.

Love from Andrew

2 January 1942

From:- Andrew Forbat 95405, RM Camp IOM
OPENED BY EXAMINER 6778
Dear Mum & Dad, Noni & John,

I cannot say how happy I was to get your letter which I got yesterday.
I would just like to point out that you can write as often as you like
& send a parcel up to 14lb. Thanks very much for the £1 which was
handed onto my Camp a/c but I think I will transfer it to Uncle Imre's
as I want to clear the debt (he paid £1 for me to the camp as I wrote
last time) as soon as possible. The parcel has not arrived yet but should
do so soon. You can be quite sure that I am as cheerful & calm as ever, &
there is absolutely no need to worry about my health or well-being. My
watch is in a shop at the very end of Blythe Road on the right hand side
as you walk up from Olympia towards Shepherd's Bush Road. In fact
it is practically at the corner of Blythe Road and Shep'ds B. Road. The
number of the watch is 237999 & the repair costs 7/6. I took it there
on 19th September 1941. Please send me also some of the books & files
from the second & third drawers of the small chest near the window of
my room. Uncle Imre is very worried because he had no news from
Edith Néni[28] yet. Ask her to telegraph or otherwise quickly let him
know of her well being. We had quite a pleasant Xmas time & the food
we got was almost luxurious. Both on the 24th and the 25th we got
some free beer & I had some too, but do not start worrying I shall not
become a drunkard. I am very sorry too that I could not see Johnny
during the Xmas holidays & I miss you all very much. Apropos, will you
get my 'Scout' from Smith's of West Ken station every Thursday & send
it also the 2 or 3 copies, which I did not have since internment. I must
close now but I shall write again next week.

Lots of love, kisses & best wishes from
Andrew

6 January 1942

OPENED BY EXAMINER 7106

All my dearest darlings,

I received your letter of the 26th yesterday & was very happy that you are all right although tired. Please write as much as you possibly can. I want to hear from you often. I did not receive the Xmas cards which John mentions, or the slippers. Last Friday we all went to the pictures for the first time & saw Charles Boyer in 'Hold back the Dawn'. It was quite a nice picture. To-day I wrote to the Principal of Chelsea Polytechnic & asked him to apply for me at t[h]e Home Office, according to §21 of the White Paper issued last year for Germans & Italians. Another young man did the same & it seems most likely that he will be released very soon, & I am confident that my time here will not be too long. Yesterday I received 7/- wages for the last two weeks for the clerical work which I have been doing. The weather here is very nice really & although it often freezes at night, it is surprisingly warm during the day. Please do not worry if you get no news for some time. I write regularly, but it takes a long time for the letters to go through the censorship, sometimes a week or more. Please send the letters I receive from other people after me. I received Tom's letter and I answered it. I should like to know what steps you have taken to help me & with what results. I am of course doing all in my power. Don't worry & wait in confidence, as I do here.

Love to everybody from Andrew.
I shall write again this week.

12 January 1942

OPENED BY EXAMINER 7106
Dearest Mum, Dad, Noni,

I was very happy with your letter of the 3rd inst. which I received to-day. I received the parcel containing suit, slippers bedlinen & chocolate on Saturday and I am very grateful for it all. The chocolate was very nice (I have still some left) and it was a wonderful feeling t[o] look like a 'gentleman' once more in my new suit. Everybody notices it, & I introduced myself as Andrew Forbat medical student (the others being AF. Internee). Will you please thank all the people who take such an interest in me in my name. I have received all your letters, although very late & all your parcels. I am all right & sufficiently warm & some people say that I look better now than before internment! Imre bácsi[30] is not too depressed, as he is kept busy with the cooking. All the Hungarian internees who are here including Aldor[31] though I do not speak much to him. I do not want anything except ties, cufflinks, Brylcreem, more chocolate if possible, & also cigarettes through a retailer for Imre bácsi. There is not much new, except that we had a 'Parliamentary crisis' yesterday, but after a lot of excitement it was solved very satisfactorily. I am missing you a lot too, but I am hoping in confidence & cheerfulness for a very early release.

Lots of love & millions of kisses to share from your Andrew

15 January 1942

OPENED BY EXAMINER 7106
My darlings,

I really cannot complain about not receiving letters for I got 8 letters during the last 2 days, many from Scouts, 1 from John, & yours of the 8th & 9th (continuing on 11-1-42). Please thank Mr. Eve for his interest and Mr. Hawkins, flat 93 for his letter. Unfortunately I cannot answer them for the present, but I shall try in following weeks. Next week I have to write to Mr. Young as he and three other Scouts wrote, so the best I can do is to write Mr. Eve the following week. The weather is quite nice here except for the last 2 days when we had such a wind that it was not safe for ships to go on the sea. Do you think Charles & Jean can do anything for me? If possible urge an application from the Polytechnic for now that the term has begun <u>every day counts</u>. You can write to me in any language so that Noni can wrote too. I am getting on well, am in good health & have so much to do now that I am never bored. My spirits stand up to the circumstances and I follow the English motto 'Make the best of it'. I am doing a lot of English teaching with Peter. I shall write again next week.

Love & kisses from
Andrew

15 January 1942

Dearest Mum, Dad & Noni,

I am writing my only letter this week (the other goes to Mr. Young) now. Because I have important news. The Intelligence officers came to us, and distributed the Application forms. However, he advised students not to apply but ask their Principals to certify to the Home Office that a British student in similar circumstances would be allowed to continue his studies and that it is desirable for him to do so. I have already written a letter to that effect, but I'd like you to make sure that he does write that Application immediately. So if possible see him or if not his Secretary, Mr. Robertshaw. It is of the utmost importance that this should be done without delay. Personally I am well. Today for the first time we heard the radio news bulletins, & we have a table tennis equipment too. I am doing little swotting as I am very busy during the day with the typing correcting, composing translating letters and applications. Besides this we (Peter & I) do a lot of teaching. Advanced students & lead the discussion class. I hope you are all well & tell about me to John as I cannot write him separately. So urge the application and don't overwork.

Lots of love & ever so many kisses from Andrew

22 January 1942

OPENED BY EXAMINER 9126
Dearest everybody,

By the time this letter arrives, you will probably have been visited by Mr, Brodszky, the famous composer, who was just released. The three Bernsteins left also to-day & Mrs. Bernstein will write to you. As glad as I am that Peter is free, I must say I shall miss him a terrible lot. Nevertheless, I shall be all the busier, for now I have taken on his job as clerk. That is to say I have to attend to the Officer in charge of our House, and I think he likes me. The new Camp leader is Count E. Zichy instead of Mr. Bernstein. Thanks for your letter of the 13th, and the 10/-. I shall buy three shirts so I shall want some more money please. I got a letter from John to-day. I am also getting letters nearly every day from my Scout friends & I had one from Robin Back recently. Please do everything possible regarding my release as I might lose a <u>whole year</u> if I am kept here for another few weeks. Above all I want to know what you have done – you can discuss it freely in your letter. Please thank Mr. Hawkins for his letters to me, I am sorry I cannot write to him. Send my watch.

Lots of love & thousands of kisses from your
Andrew

23 March 1942 – after a long gap of missing letters

Dear Everybody,

I am glad that Andy is so satisfied with my exam results, and I hope that you are too, so will I get my long trousers? As I really was second.

Any way, Tommy wrote and told me that if you don't buy me long trousers then <u>he will</u> and I am sure you don't want that! Do you?

I have written to Mrs. P. yesterday so I am expecting a reply some time this week.

We had our R.S.A. arithmetic exam on Friday and I think I'll pass (just about).

I shall be coming home on Wednesday April 1st on the 4.6 p.m. train straight after school & I'll arrive in London at 8.00 p.m.

What do you think of the amount raised for London Warship Week? I think its grand.

Well I am really looking foreward to seeing you all in just over one weeks time and I am looking foreward to that Easter Camp.

After next week I shall be getting 5/- a week for my papers and have to do 2 more. So I'll be rich.

I have now 6/6 in the savings.

Tommy said that when I shall be home for Easter he will phone me up, all this will be arranged beforehand.

I am just about jumping with eagerness, at the thought of seeing you so soon.

Well I'll pack up now as I am going down town to get some chips.

Lots of love & kisses from your everloving
John

P.S. Give my love to Noni.

P.P.S. I am sending the Postal Order back as it has to be cashed in Fulham so you must cash it and buy another one and send it to me.

P.T.O. [More shorthand on the back.]

25 March 1942

Dear Everybody,

I am just writing this short note as I have to send my report. It is included in this letter, and I hope you will be satisfied with it.

Officially I came third but really I came second because there were two top boys.

So please buy me some long trowsers.

Well there is nothing much to write now as I wrote yesterday so good-by, hoping to see you in a week (Wednesday 8 o' clock).

Lots of love & kisses from your everloving
John

P.S. Send my fares at once <u>John</u> please

Notes from Father

[Uncle] Imre was released [from internment] toward the end of April [1942] and of course I immediately gave him my place. I left the Pop Inn again and for the last time. Since I had no job, I went to the Labour Exchange, that I wanted a position as a clerk. I received an unemployment allowance, of 25/- or 28/- [shillings] a week, for which I had to stand in line twice a week to have my card stamped. They could not find a job for me and in the end they told me to go to a Government Training Course, where they would train me as a toolmaker and that would qualify me to work in a munitions factory. During the course I would get 65/- a week. I had no choice in the matter, I had to accept it and shortly I took my place as an apprentice. I had to rise at 6 a.m. to get there on time, or even earlier because we had to clock in when I arrived and clock out when I left. I was not late once. They gave me work clothes, an overall and that is how they started to teach me to file steel. I never realised how hard it was to be a steel worker. I could hardly lift the big rusty steel plates, from which I had to cut a piece with hammer and chisel, to clean them down with Emery paper and then file out the prescribed pattern. The instructor saw that I was struggling for an hour to split off a piece from the metal plate, it would not split and I did not have enough strength for it. He asked what have I been doing for so long. When I told him, he set to it with hammer and chisel, and what I could not do in hours, he completed in three minutes. There were all sorts of men around me, mostly working-class, but also two foreign lawyers and others.

I do not know why, my workmates treated me with respect. We had to sweep the floors ourselves at the end of the workday and one of my mates took the broom out of my hand by force, saying he would do it instead of me. I protested, saying it was my job. When the instructor saw that he was trying to do it instead of me, he said 'this is your job, do it yourself'. I told him it was not my intention to push my work on another and that my mate was too polite toward me (he was a trumpeter in civilian life) and started sweeping myself. Soon the instructor returned and said, 'hand the broom to your friend, I cannot stand seeing it in your hands, somehow it does not suit you'. Everyone was addressed by his surname, Smith, Brown, etc., they called me Mr. Forbat. No matter, how much I protested that I did not want to be an exception; they set me apart without looking down at me. Everyone was remarkably helpful and polite toward me. Despite my efforts I could not file evenly, and could not make hair-line accurate angles and the work made me dead tired. When I returned after a break in the canteen, where I had horrible lunch or dinner, I lay down on the lawn and said to myself, 'God why don't you allow me to die, why must I suffer this deadly fatigue?' But I did not complain to Mum.

I had no difficulty with the theoretical instruction. I understood it better than most of the others and as bad as my manual work was despite my best effort, I knew my theory. When a new man came to learn, the instructor entrusted him to me to explain the different kinds of tools and how one had to copy the drawings on to the steel plate, etc. 'You know these better than I do,' he said. After about six weeks, my colleagues had learnt the trade and one after the other got jobs in factories. My turn did not come, three, four and five months later I was still there and they did not offer me a job. I started getting stomach pains from the strenuous work and I felt that my stomach trouble was returning. I went to see the Labour Exchange doctor and asked him to examine me. He concluded that I was not suitable for heavy manual work, he gave me a certificate which I showed to the management and they gave me a discharge. No doubt they were pleased to be rid of me seeing that I was completely useless in this kind of work. They gave me a beautiful testimonial, praising my punctuality, industry, reliability and I departed with that in my pocket. I was 'free' again, but without a job and income. I returned to alternate between the Pop Inn and the Lederer bridge club, and returned to the Labour Exchange seeking a job and getting unemployment help, but I did not find a job.

1 June 1942

Dear Mum, Dad, Andrew & Noni,

I safely arrived in Melksham at about 8.40 p.m. wher[e] Bill was waiting Jim and me. He took or kits ons his bike so it saved us from having to carry them home. I did my round & went to school as usual to-day and also I went to typing. Also later on I'll very likely go gardenning.

I've already paid for my shoes so that matter is settled. There is no news here so I'll say cheerio! From your everloving

John

6 June 1942

Dear Mum & Dad,

Thanks very much for your letter. Was ever so happy to hear that Mum is better. The other day I had a parcel from Tommy in which was a lively book a big Scout book. As when I got back to Melksham, guess what I was told. I am the P.L. of the Kingfisher Patrol what do you think of that? But Andy please don't tell anyone in the 10th as they'll only laugh. Please send me my toothbrush & my coupons at once, as I am going to buy myself some bathing trunks out of my savings.

Lots of love & kisses from your everloving
John

21 July 1942

Dear Everybody,

Thanks very much for your card which I got to-day. Thanks Andy for making arrangements about 1st class journey. Don't forget to reserve me a ground sheet. I hope Dad is getting on OK with work & I'm sorry that Mum is so tired. I am terribly excited about seeing you so soon.

I am sending Andy's groundsheet so that he can have it for camp. The blankets I'll bring with me so that they will be ready for camp. Please send 6/- for my shoes.

Lots of love & kisses from your everloving
John

August 1942 – from both boys at Scout summer camp
10th Fulham Scout Camp,
Thorpe Estate,
Rosemary Lane,
Thorpe,
Surrey

Dear Mum & Dad,

Just a line to tell you that I am getting on fine & enjoying camp as ever. At first the weather was not too brilliant, but we have just had two nice hot days & we were swimming in a little pond.

I have written to John, but to make sure, tell him to bring the tent we have & my dissecting set with him when he comes to camp.

Meals are quite good here, & I have done my share of cooking too. Just so that Noni should be pleased tell that we got up at seven o' clock every morning, & the first thing we do is to wash & have breakfast, & we have to do our own washing up. Talking of washing will you send an extra towel for me with John, as the present one is rather dirty An extra washcloth would do no harm either, if you can spare it. I am sorry to say that my fountain pen has not turned up either.

I hope you are not working too hard, & Daddy is making nice things[32] without getting very tired. I'd better close now, as we are going swimming.

Lots of love to everybody including Noni, Sheila[33] *& all the family of uncles, aunts cousins etc. With still more love to you from*
Andrew

6 August 1942

Dear Mum & Dad & Noni,

I am enclosing my birthday greetings for Daddy. I am sorry that John cannot write on it, but he is on his first class hike & I must post this now so that it should be with you tomorrow.

There is no news, so give my love to everybody from Andrew

…continued by Andrew

My darling Daddy,

It is a pity that I cannot be there to wish you a most happy birthday personally, but I promise that you will get my birthday kisses all right, only a day too late.

Another year of worry, another year of trouble, sorrow, blood, tears, sweat and toil has passed. The struggle was hard and weary. Yet you bore it in high spirits, in good temper and a cheerful grin; you did not flinch, you did not fail, you did not despair. All I have to ask the Almighty, that this birthday might mark the end of this struggle, that in years to come, you may find the reward of your toil, that the wrinkles of worry on your forehead may be smoothened by years of happiness, that you may find pleasure and satisfaction from life, that the family you sustained for 20 long years may repay your effort and that your life should be long and the road to the end should be strewn with flowers of love and bliss, and free from the shadows of worry and sorrow.

That is the wish of your everloving son Andrew

An Impossible Child

My lucrative paperboy era was severely interrupted when impetigo rashes and scabs began to cover enough of my body for teachers to send me to the doctor. Highly contagious and capable of becoming an agent of germ warfare, I was soon denied contact with the newspaper delivery industry and when 100 per cent of my body became covered, I was sent to hospital for more intensive treatment. Not the most pleasant of procedures: nurses would apply hot Kaolin poultices to my various rashes, including on my private parts. When the poultices had cooled, dried and firmly stuck to my skin, they were unceremoniously ripped off, taking the scabs with them. Numerous repetitions over about a week gradually eliminated the disease and, with firm instructions to make good use of Carbolic soap, I was let loose again somewhat blotchy but apparently cured. Maybe I really was an 'impossible' child!

24 October 1942

Dear Everybody,

I got your letter this morning and just after I went to the Hospital to let them know that I had not gone home when I got there I was told to wait for the doctor when he came he had a look at me and said I should have to stay in Hospital and now here I am in the Men's Ward. The doctor said that I shall be in here for about 10 day to a fortnight. I am feeling quite all right so don't worry. It is a very nice Hospital with nice nurses and sisters. Please send some more Almás Pite.[34] I am sending my clothes coupons so please try to buy me a pair of pyjamas and I desperately need som[e] trousers and a jacket as this suit needs a wash very badly. I am now pretty well covered with starch poultices which until they are dry are very slimy. Mr. Robbins is in the same ward as I am as he has a poisoned leg and has been in her for over a week. Mts. Robbins will soon be here I suppose and then she will post this letter.

I don't know anything about this allolution [sic] yet but I shall ask. For the last week I have been sleeping alone. Ruby did have Impetigo just after I did but it was not catching so I don't think I got it from her.

How are you all getting on? I also enclose my report and you will see that I came 4th, which Dr. Cavell puts down to my absence from school for a while.

I have no more to write now but I am longing to see you all so cheerio for now from your everloving

John

P.S. Please send some money.

A Lecture

Notwithstanding my much-improved school exam results – near the top of my class in which I was the youngest by two years – the following admonishing letter was received by me from Andrew who was then a second year medical student. Of course, my poor English (spelling and punctuation) was self-evident from the letters.

26 October 1942

My dear Johnny,

I am sorry to see from your letter that your impetigo is still not getting better, but hope that with the hospital treatment you are getting, your recovery will not be long delayed. While you are in hospital, I hope you are not wasting your time. It is more essential now than ever before that you should make some progress in your schoolwork which I am afraid is more like the standard of a 12 year old secondary school boy than of a 14 year old.

Your report is not bad, but by no means as good as it might be. I am not worried about your low book-keeping mark, although of course it is desirable that you should be good in everything. On the other hand, great and immediate improvement is needed especially in English and Mathematics, and considering the standard you are working on, in French.

Let us take the subjects one by one. Your English must not be neglected on any account, because whatever you go, whatever job you apply for as good and correct English is a great asset, but a faulty loose Cockney creates a very bad impression. I expect that beside Grammar your spelling let you down badly. I find far too many common words spelt wrongly in your letters. Whenever you read printed matter watch how the words are spelt. After all, you are a Scout and your observation should be quite good. Just remember that next time.

I do not know why you are so weak in Maths. I have told you before that an Engineer must know a great deal of Maths well, and unless you understand the elementary principles thoroughly now, you will never be able to understand more difficult things like calculus. Get an elementary text-book on arithmetic algebra and geometry, and workout as many problems as possible. Do not look at the answer until you have made a <u>really</u> honest attempt at working out, & if you still cannot get it right, I am sure Dr. Cavell will be only too pleased to help you. Do not think I am trying to talk you into becoming a 'swot' although there are many things far worse than that which you might become. But, <u>if you want to get on in life you must give up a certain amount of your spare time now</u> otherwise you will never become anything. Moreover, the more you learn, the greater the fascination will become to learn more. If you do not <u>try</u> to become interested you never will. Do you remember when I told you a few things about Biology? How you wanted more and more! You will find it the same with all the other subjects.

I miss you a great deal Johnny. I wish with all my heart that you were in London for good, so that I could guide you and help you in your work, with only 3 of the old masters left in the school you cannot be expected to do much. I am going to Streatham next Wednesday to enquire about getting you to a London secondary school. They are not so terribly expensive & at least you would get a decent education.

By the way, do not kid yourself into thinking that the education you get is anywhere near enough. I was at Westken when nearly all the masters were there, and now that I see the Secondary and Public School boys, I see how deficient <u>my</u> education has been. Unfortunately your education is very far from mine, so you can get an idea how behind you are and how hard you will have to work to be better than the rest. So not be discouraged, because that work will be enjoyable and in the end when you have achieved your aims you will appreciate the fruits of your labour far more than if they had been 'dropped into your mouth'. Don't forget – there are no roses without thorns.

I expect that if I go on lecturing like this you will feel that you do not want to come back to London at all, but what I said is of the utmost importance to you and I hope you will take my words of concentrated wisdom to heart (i.e. the left and right auricles and ventricles).

As for me, I am getting on quite well now I have dissected the back, the chest, shoulder and armpit, taken the arm off and starting on the arm now. Although we have a fair amount to learn, I am enjoying myself.

At Scouts things are going much the same as usual. I still run parades until Mr. Young comes down on the whole the boys behave themselves. You will see from the bulletin that Les Fielder has been promoted P.L. – and I think you know the rest. I shall ask Mr. Young for your Missioner's and Cooks Badge when I next see him. I have the green-all-rounds here & will send the whole lot together – or you can come and collect them yourself – I hope soon.

I have not much more to say now so I'd better pack up. Otherwise I shall find myself writing a book to you instead of a letter. In the meanwhile you can be working these out & send me the answers next time:-

Divide $3x + 5$ into $6x^3 - 5x^2 + 8x - 6$

If $T = 2\varpi\sqrt{K/MH}$ find an expression for M

Find the factors of $8a^3 - 1/27b^3$

The hypotenuse of a right angled triangle is 8cms. and the base is 3cms. find the perpendicular showing how you work out the square root. (Do not use logarithms for this one)

A, B & C are in partnership. A having a capital of £5,000, B of £4,000 and C of £3,000. If the net profit they make is 17% of the total capital, show how much profit each should receive, if the profit is distributed in ration of the capitals contributed.

In all these problems show working unless you have done it in your head. If you cannot do the algebra, take a book and look the parts considered up. They are not difficult.

Best of luck & speedy recovery & lots of love from
Andrew

4

Life and Limb in Wartime London

No later 'evacuation letters' have survived. I recovered from the impetigo and was able to resume my newspaper deliveries job at W.H. Smith. As air raids seemed to be declining after three years of evacuation, it was agreed that I should finally and permanently return home to London at the end of 1942 – as it turned out, just in time for a resumption of regular night raids.

Labelled by our doctor as a 'septic child' on account of recurring boils and similar signs of vitamin C deficiency, he recoiled from my fingers that now reeked of aeroplane 'dope' arising from enthusiastic model building. Now 14 and no longer so puny, I was soon issued with the obligatory steel helmet and navy blue 'Fire Guard' armband in gold lettering, for duties in the six-storey block of flats, where we now lived. I still had to share a bedroom, sleeping on a mattress while Andrew slept on the base of one divan and my grandmother Noni had a second divan to herself – with her chamber pot close by. Ignoring our proper bathroom, she insisted on treating us to the sounds and odours of her chamber music and it was quite a relief to get up in the night for fireguard duty. This involved patrolling the corridors to check for incendiary bombs and, more interestingly, standing on the flat roof

John's original fireguard armband. (Author's collection)

above the sixth floor to watch the search lights pick out bombers and to see the anti-aircraft shells bursting.

Regular training and practice in the art of extinguishing incendiary bombs with the piddling jet from a stirrup pump in a bucket of water was quite fun. We were taught to crawl beneath the smoke and to direct the jet, holding the hose over our heads while another pumped, 'til the bucket was empty. I was ready to go to bed one evening some hours before my watch duty time, when a raid was going, 'ding dong', as I watched the action over North End Road through the window, with the blackout curtains behind me. A stick of bombs started whistling towards us from the north, each a little nearer, and when the whistling reached shrieking level I ducked back behind the curtain. The bomb fell a short distance away and the window I had been looking through shredded the curtain at stomach level. Soon the chief of our fireguard section was ringing our doorbell:

'John, take this pink form to the Auxiliary Fire Station at Beaufort Street School and tell them we need them to put out a fire on the corner of Gliddon Road. We already pulled an old lady out – except she insisted on going back for her false teeth. Be quick now.'

By now having my own bike, earned by tilling Uncle Eugene's allotment for 1/- a day, I donned my 'tin hat' and, clutching the pink form sped the half-mile along North End Road, crunched over never-ending broken glass. When I arrived, the school itself was well alight. 'Go back son, we're busy putting out our own fire,' was the disappointing outcome. Miraculously without the tyres going flat, I made the return ride over the glass and the fire in Gliddon Road just continued to burn.

Bombsites were everywhere and they provided free planks, from which I was able to construct my Scout patrol's own storage cupboard. Screwing them together without the benefit of drills to make way for the screws I had scrounged meant the palms of my hands were covered in blisters. This sturdy piece of furniture was then painted and placed in our St Andrews Hall Scout headquarters. On Scout nights it was brought out to our patrol corner, where my Buffaloes Patrol lined up for 'colours' and inspection, before taking out our manuals, ropes and first-aid bandages, for instruction in everything from compass and mapping work, signalling, treating burns and fractures, to the Scout law and the Scout Promise.

These periods were interspersed with team games requiring quick thinking, lots of running and jumping and the absolute favourite – British Bulldog. With boys' ages ranging from 11, through to hefty 17- and 18-year-olds nearly ready for military call-up, the game started with one boy in the middle of the hall and everybody else at one end. On the signal, we had to run to the other end and try to avoid being caught and lifted off the ground by the one in the middle. Once thus caught, we remained in the middle and helped to stop the rush on the next signal to run back. Each catch involved a lively struggle and gradually the number of runners reduced 'til eventually a last one remained, to brave the gauntlet through the whole troop barring the way in the middle. This would be one of the biggest, toughest lads and, by the time I was 16 or so, I prided myself on getting through more than once. Mother fulfilled the all-too-frequent duty of resuscitating my uniform to patrol inspection standards.

Like most boys, I was sometimes late for school. Everybody was late sometimes and at assembly, after the headmaster had announced who had been killed in the previous night's raids, the late boys were paraded for their punishment. As a Jewish boy, I was excused attending

Doodlebugs over the Law Courts, London. (By kind permission of Mr Phillip Jarrett)

assembly without suffering any cultural or other traumas. When I became a prefect, and it was customary for prefects to take turns at reading the lesson, I joined in and read from the Old Testament. I still demurred from joining in the prayers and, sitting on the prefects' bench, the other kids joined in the joke when they saw my hymnbook held accidentally-on-purpose upside down.

I must have been 15 when the doodlebug flying bombs began to rain down at all hours. One of the first passed right over our heads as

Andrew and I were cycling into Kent one Friday evening for one of our many weekend Scout camps. The A2 ran dead-straight south-east and the throaty ramjet roared ever louder as it approached to fly, rather low, directly overhead. Flak was bursting all around it – quite a spectacular show – 'til the shrapnel started to bounce off the pavement around us and we ducked into a doorway, later burning our fingers collecting the hot shards.

On the way home on Sunday, we passed the Streatham house of a good friend who was old enough to have been called up for Service. Their front door was missing and all their windows were blown in, so Mrs Randall asked us to go to her sister who lived near us in London, to tell her they were OK. We got back onto our bikes and passed the cause of the Randalls' damage – a whole block of houses flattened by a single doodlebug, leaving little more than a big crater. We cycled on past our flats towards the Randalls' relatives in Hammersmith and, racing north as the sirens wailed, we heard another throaty roar rapidly approaching. We had been trained to wait until the engine cut, then to lie down in the gutter with our hands covering our heads. The doodlebugs then pitched down to dive onto wherever they were pointing. It cut out very close to us, so we leapt off our bikes, dived for the kerb and waited.

A great mushroom cloud rose where it had hit in the next street and we got back up. Before we could pass on the Randalls' message, Andrew, who had started medical school by then, tarried to render first aid. In the months while the doodlebug campaign persisted, the air-raid sirens sounded just about every few minutes. Most people ran into air-raid shelters – often down into the Underground, where at night many slept on the platforms – but as many doodlebugs came during the day as at night. Our flats had a big basement that was used as a shelter, we boys only used it to practice our table tennis, however, and it was otherwise unused. As Mother found out only after the war was over, being up on the roof was more exciting during air raids.

The frequency of air-raid warnings got so high that taking heed would completely prevent all normal activity and, for the first time in my school days, I determined *never* to be late. No way was I going to let

Sheltering from bombing in a West End London Underground station.
(Wikimedia Commons/FDR Library, New York)

Hitler dominate my life any longer! Air-raid warning or not, I rode to
Sloane school and thumbing my nose at Hitler, without fail arrived on
time every day. When the V2 rockets began to fall from their trajectory
into space, there was no warning and no way to hide anyway. Once you
heard the explosion – followed by the whine of its supersonic arrival –
it was obvious that some other poor bastard had bought it.

Notes from Father

I wrote more applications, tried with the BBC without success. I listened to some of the Hungarian broadcasts and I did not like them and shared my objections. They thanked me, asked me to follow their broadcasts with attention and to pass on my observations. Since, as an enemy alien I was not allowed to possess a radio, I wrote to the Home Office, asked them to change my enemy alien status, since my every personal interest was tied to the British State, and I enclosed my correspondence with the BBC. One morning, they called me to the police and the officer said: 'You want a radio?' I replied that that was a peripheral question, I do not want to be an enemy alien and then I would automatically be able to have a radio. He was very unfriendly, interrogated me in detail about my family and everything else. When he asked about Uncle Eugene, I said he was English. Sarcastically he replied, 'He is only naturalized British, he will not be English as long as he lives.' I was upset by the unusual lack of courtesy on the part of the police and when he said I could have a radio if I wanted to, but they would not change my status as enemy alien, I said, thank you, then I do not want a radio either.

By this time, Andrew had finished his preliminary studies at Chelsea Polytechnic and he had to find a place in a medical school. We went from one hospital to another, sent applications with the very best test scores and recommendation from wherever he had studied, but all said that they had no more vacancies. Finally I got [him] an interview with the Dean of the Guy's Hospital Medical School, who said that they had one position for which there were seven or eight applicants. They would hold an examination and the best would get the place. Andrew took the test and he was among the first twelve for whom there were places. The Dean informed me regretfully, that I should understand that they had to give preference to English applicants. It seemed hopeless for our poor son to be able to continue his studies. The next day there was an unexpected message from University College, where Andrew had also applied, that one of their applicants had withdrawn and they would accept Andrew. This was an unexpected bit of luck and we were now at peace that our son could become a doctor. The college was evacuated to Leatherhead, about an hour from London. Since we did not have money to get him lodgings there, he travelled there daily. As the bombing became lighter and the war was becoming more hopeful, we wanted to bring Johnny home as well, to the regret of his teachers who were very fond of him. I went to the principal of a school in London – it was not free, one had to pay a small tuition fee – and when I showed him Johnny's report and recommendations from his teachers, he decided that they would admit Johnny for the following term to begin three months later. So, we would all be together again after Christmas.

Poor thing, Mum left the house early to open the Pop Inn and I stayed at home with her mother. Sometimes she cooked my mid-day dinner and I did not like it. She could not cook nearly as wonderfully as Mum, since she, with her precision, was transformed into a most outstanding cook by then. I was prejudiced against her mother's pride of being Italian. I hated Italians as much as I knew in my feelings since the Italians who were our allies before the First World War, stabbed us in the back, and attacked us and now also, on the other side in the Second World War.

One evening I went home, thinking that Mum would already be there, but she was not. I waited a while, then I went down to the Underground station across the road. One train came after another – without her. When she was not in the last one, I got very anxious. I phoned the Pop Inn, with the knowledge that there would be no reply, since at that time it was usually closed. To my surprise, Uncle Eugene answered. There was something peculiar in his voice and manner of speaking. He said, there was nothing special, but Mum was not feeling well and they put her on the sofa until she felt better. I could not imagine what her trouble could be, I was restless, but Uncle Eugene said that she was better, I should wait at home and he would bring Mum home shortly. I walked up and down like a madman outside the gate, went up to the flat, went down again until at last at 2:30 a.m. a taxi drew up at the by the gate. Uncle Eugene and a strange woman emerged and they lifted Mum out. Uncle Eugene tried to calm me down that there was no trouble. She was deadly pale and could not speak or stand on her feet. That is how we took her upstairs, undressed her and put her to bed. It came out that Mum had collapsed, she had hardly any pulse, her heart *was racing like on one occasion before Andrew was born when we were frightened. The three and a half years of excessive work twelve hours daily and sometimes more, standing on her feet the whole day had taken their toll. The woman with her was a stranger, who happened to be in the Pop Inn; since she was a nurse, she took care of her. She stayed the night; the three of us lay dressed in the bed, until slowly she came to herself. Next day the doctor came early in the morning and ordered complete peace and rest. In a few days, with God's help Mum collected yourself and I decided that she would leave the work at the Pop Inn.*

30 July 1944 – from Scout camp near Thorpe, Surrey

My darlings,

Just a line to let you know that I am well. John has not arrived yet (4 p.m.) but I will get him to add a few words when he does.

I was rather late getting here, because I got a puncture on the way, & my attempts to mend it were not successful. I did not walk. I rode on a flat tyre & thus my progress was somewhat slower.

We had quite a bit of sunshine this morning, but it is pouring with rain now. Of course we are quite dry inside the tents. I am writing sitting on the Ambulance Kit as a chair & a patrol-box as a table & the store-tent as my office.

There is no more news as yet, except that I have examined nearly every boy's chest.

With love to all, with special regards to Noni,
Lots of kisses
Andrew

… continued by John

Dear Mum & Dad,

I arrived O.K. at about 5 o' clock and I'm having a good time. We play cricket a lot and we are going into Windsor this afternoon probably for swimming.

Cheerio & love to all,
John

5 August 1944

My darling Daddy,

The closer two people are together the more difficult it is to express birthday wishes adequately. Conventional phrases are sufficient for acquaintances and very convenient – yet common use has subtracted from their value so that they remain but convenient phrases.

Today I find it as difficult as every to put down into words my birthday wishes. But the wishes are the same, old, good and fine ones all of which point in the same general direction – true happiness. Then I wish you all the things which will make you happy, love from your beloved ones, health of body, and personal comfort of mind, body and soul. And I hope that all things which will make you less happy – grief, worry, anxiety will keep far far away from you.

In the past year or so, God has been more gracious to us all. He has allowed us to recover financially to a certain degree – for this we thank Him. May this progress continue. But even as, financial and social state belongs to the superficial things which make up happiness, you know more than I do that our family life was very happy when our pockets were very poor. Equally you know many rich people who are unhappy. So my desire is that our home life shall continue to be happy in the future as it has always been in the past. Let us look to each other with the love and respect that meant so much in the past. There is no disagreement which love cannot bridge and if we remember that I see no reason why ever there should be a gap between us. I d[o] not believe that there is one now and I hope there never will be.

At this time of the year I like to remember the debt I owe to you. I have no hesitation in reaffirming my promise – one that I have made several times – that if I have anything to do with it at all there should be no reason for you or Mother to have financial worries once I am established in my profession. I hope my letter is not too disjointed – as I said before it is difficult to describe one's feelings truly. All the same the good wish goes out. Many happy, healthy and long life for my Father.

Love and a million 'puszi'[85]
from Andrew

... *continued by John*

My dear dad,

This just a line to wish you the happiest birthday and coming year that any King can hope for, let alone you. That you live happily in health and in love with your dear ones for man[y] many more years to come. I am afraid this is a very poor birthday greeting but I hope you realise that my feelings are affectionate towards you and my loyalty to you as a son will always be true.

Love and everything good from
John

Flying for Boys

If only I could be a couple of years older – I would have given my right arm to fly a Spitfire like some of my brother's friends. Finding an old wingless biplane in a farm shed outside Melksham when we were evacuated away from London and our family was a major coup. Safe from prying eyes, a friend and I would climb into the tandem cockpits and waggle the joystick, making engine and machine-gun noises till we were hoarse.

The nearest I could get to this was in the Air Training Corps, which camped us at an RAF station for a fortnight each year. Yes, there was the interminable square bashing on the parade ground and eating in the airmen's mess off tin plates, which had to be washed in a trough of boiling water on the way out. Too bad if you dropped a knife in – it had to be retrieved. Yes, kit inspections in our Nissen hut quarters were a chore, as we made neat stacks with the three 'biscuits' that constituted our mattresses and polished our boots. But we had sessions in the simulators with real bomb sights, pretending to drop bombs on dimly lit German targets – and then finally the real thing, a four-hour operational training flight in a four-engined Sterling bomber. Wearing flying suits and parachutes

A Short Sterling bomber. (Public information)

An RAF Tigermoth. (By kind permission of Mr Phillip Jarrett)

like the real airmen, we experienced high-altitude bombing on the range and machine-gunning at buoys from low altitude over the Wash.

Four hours was the minimum to qualify us for a 'flying meal' of two eggs with bacon and sausages – my favourite, at a time when egg rationing only allowed each member of our family one teaspoonful from Dad's specially permitted egg ration for those with an ulcer. Unfortunately, corkscrew evasive manoeuvres to escape a mock fighter attack halfway through this adventure got the better of my stomach and I spent the last two hours retching into the Elsan in the rear, leaving no stomach for my coveted flying meal.

16 July 1945 – from Air Training Corps camp

Dear Mum,

Well here I am & I am having quite a good time. The food is O.K. & the whole thing is quite interesting. I had a short flight yesterday and piloted the 'plane for a while. We should fly again several times in the week.

Well, how are you enjoying your holiday? I hope you go out & see the sights. It should be nice there. Go and see the lakes and the mountains etc.

I am sorry I was late in phoning on Friday. Everything was all right and I had a lovely flight, about 30 minutes we did some aerobatics, and I took over for about 10 minutes.

Well cheerio for now and have a good time. Write & tell me how you like the place.

Cheerio & love from
John

Low Hops

Even more sought after was everybody's ambition: the gliding course, when we would really learn to fly. The January to April 1945 period was not the best for weather, but there were enough hours over a number of weekends to get some excitement. Trouble was that there were only single-seat gliders, requiring us to fly solo from the first attempt. Today, this is regarded with horror by flyers and lay people alike, but then it was the norm and we were soon being winched across Hounslow Heath – long before it became Heathrow.

The Dagling looked not unlike the first Wright gliders; a pair of wings mounted high above a keel carrying a tail, a seat, joystick and rudder bar – all out in the fresh air. Initially with spoilers on the wings, we were strapped on and hauled rapidly towards the winch, bumping along the ground, learning to keep our wings level and to use the rudder without dipping them into the ground. Once mastered, the spoilers came off and we could take off for short flights low over the heath. This was beginning to get somewhere.

Next came the best part: converting to a higher performance machine, the Kirby Cadet. This actually sported a fuselage – still with an open cockpit and without instruments or wheels. Low hops started with two boys holding the wing tips and the instructor squatting down to be level with my face. He reached in to the joystick and said, 'Hold it about there.

John flying the Dagling solo. (Author's collection)

Off you go.' Thus ended the lesson and the winch hauled me along until the wing boys could not keep up. Now in control, I did what every boy of 16 who always wanted to fly would do – pulled back hard. The Kirby Cadet responded like a bird and leapt skywards, presenting me with this unfamiliar horizon situated well down below the nose, the ground rapidly receding. 'Wow! I'm going up too fast!' I pushed down smartly – causing the horizon to leap up high, as we rushed towards the ground. I pulled up again, repeating the first leap and then breathlessly down again as the glider porpoised across Hounslow Heath. After two or three such switch backs, the winch operator stopped pulling and coaxed me back to a reasonably soft landing. I had done a 50ft-high low hop.

Since much of the day was spent retrieving gliders from the winch end to the launch point for other cadets, the next try was on another day. The porpoising effect was somewhat reduced as my 'pump handling' motions smoothed out. After a few more low hops I could cleanly climb to 50ft, put the nose down and glide down to land. Now we were ready for high hops to 100ft – about the height of a ten-storey building.

Confidence abundant, I could snatch the wing tips from the wing boys' grip as they ran along and made the takeoff, except the Cadet kept

A Kirby Cadet. (By kind permission of Mr Phillip Jarrett)

An Auster like the one John flew. (By kind permission of Mr Phillip Jarrett)

climbing till the winch operator and I thought I had reached the 100ft altitude. Then I could put the nose down, pull the plug to release the cable and glide down, absolutely free and on my own. This was the real thing! A modicum of further advice came from the instructor below if I tried to 'stretch' the glide, when he cupped his hands to his mouth and shouted a barely audible 'stick forward'. Near the final weekend, instead of spending much of the time between flights retrieving gliders for other cadets, we were allowed to make two consecutive flights, rather than when flights separated by days or even a week, in order to better get our hand in and learn. For my first high hop, the instructor told me he would stand well down the flight path and I would have to land near him. This went fine as I landed some 20yd to one side of him – into a good enough wind to keep my wings level without the help of wing boys. 'Right. Now make your second high hop – but this time, land nearer to me.'

At 100ft altitude the instructor looked about 2ft tall, and on releasing the cable I put the nose down and headed straight for him. At 50ft, he began walking to my left and with a little left rudder, he was lined up

A Glider retrieving Falcon 3. (By kind permission of Mr Phillip Jarrett)

with my nose again. Soon he began walking to my right and with total confidence and a little right rudder, he was back in my sights. This was fun. When I was within about 15ft from the ground, I steered a little away from him and landed smoothly, keeping my wings level until he reached my side. 'Was that near enough Sir?,' I asked. Instructors flew a full circuit up to 800ft at each day's end and on his approach, my instructor almost cut my head off.

Although nearly every glider in the school received some damage, only one incident produced casualties. On his last flight as the course was finishing, one Terry Rogers asked Athol Lonie, our flight sergeant, to take his picture during the takeoff. It was a bumpy start to a late takeoff and Lonie had not allowed for the distortions of his camera's viewfinder, but stayed in the flight path until Terry's wing leading edge sliced into his chin. At that point, Terry's glider went up vertically for a few feet, tipped over onto one wing and collapsed in a heap on the ground, breaking Terry's ankle. Lonie was left lying unconscious – but fortunately after a short stay in hospital, he had only lost a few teeth.

5 August 1945 – from 10th Fulham Scout Camp, Surrey

Dear Dad,

I am writing to you, to wish you a happy birthday. I must say it is hard to put down on paper one's feelings on such occasions but I want you to realize, how much <u>I</u> realise the debt both Andrew and I owe you (and Mother) for obviously, any son owes a great debt to his parents.

I wish from depth of my reason, that you carry on with a long, healthy and extremely happy life, together with mum and with us always close at hand to help and be helped when necessary. I am afraid I cannot put my feelings in any better form. And I think you will understand what I mean.

Please excuse my writing in pencil but my pen has run out of ink. Well cheerio for now and we shall see you soon. Love to Mum Noni & all.

Cheerio
John

August 1945 – from 10th Fulham Scout Camp, Surrey

Dear Everybody,

Thanks very much for your letter a few days ago. I'm sorry I did not write before but as I saw you not long ago there was no hurry. I am having a good time here and I wish you would come down for a day this week.

If you can come write and tell us when you are coming.

Last week we had beautiful weather although the last two days were not so good.

I am feeling fit & well and I've got plenty to eat. The only thing I miss is you. Please come down.

I went swimming to-day and swam nearly a mile, and now I am going down to the village to get some chocolate. Well I'll say cheerio now. Please come.

Yours Ever
John

P.S. Write & tell us when you will arrive.

… continued by Andrew

Lots of love from me too. Having a lovely time teaching & examining chaps & giving first aid.

See you Saturday, till then love to all,

Andrew

25 August 1946 – from 18 Church Avenue, Crosland Moor, Huddersfield,
Yorks[36]

Dear Mum, Dad & Andrew,

I am having a very nice time up here, and the people with whom I am staying, could not be kinder. They like me very much and we get on very well. The food is very good and there is plenty of it.

Well, now, I hope that has put your minds at rest.

On Wednesday, we went out for a long walk in the morning, took sandwitches with us, and returned in the evening. In all we did about 20 miles. We went right over the moors, climbing mountains, and going down in the valleys. The view was beautiful and also luckily the weather.

On the way, we found a lovely little site for camping, and so we went out on Friday and stayed till yesterday.

The place was where two lovely little rocky mountain streams meet in a little valley and there was a little wood of beech. The streams were crystal clear and very fast running, so we tested it to see if it was good for drinking, and it was. It was a really beautiful spot. The only thing wrong was that in the evening, lots of tiny flies came out and bit us and crawled over us, until we scratched like madmen.

The first day we had lovely weather, but the second it rained a few times. Still we had a really good time and plenty of good food to eat. I made some lovely chips for dinner yesterday.

On the way back it was raining and we could not get on the bus as it was full, so we started walking, but luckily some kind people gave us a lift in their car, almost all the way home.

As soon as we got in, we had a bath & changed, and had a big supper of plaice, fried potatoes etc. This morning I had a boiled egg for breakfast.

Thanks Andrew, for writing and sending on 'The Scout'. I wrote to Jean Montjotin[37] (in French). Has he sent his ticket yet, I hope everything is all right.

There seems little else for me to say except that I shall be back on Saturday. I'll let you know, at what time and where. Perhaps one of you could meet me.

I'll close now and I hope not only Andrew will reply!!!

Cheerio for now, & love to all from your
John

Moral Fibre

Throughout this period and for years to come, the character and leadership training inherent in being a Scout stood me in ever greater stead. Working up through Patrol Leader, Troop Leader and King's Scout with a surfeit of merit badges, Scouting was more a part of my life even than the Air Training Corps.

At school, between occasional runs into the air-raid shelter, we manfully joked about the difference between a Gestapo agent and a Russian policeman – the latter being a Rostov Tech and the former, a Malapropism reversal, into a 'tossed off wreck'. Mr Nightingale, our eccentric mathematics teacher, proved his reputed madness by deftly drawing large, perfect, freehand circles on the blackboard, then wiping it clean with his tattered black master's gown after geometry was over. 'This must have cost at least £6,' (a lot of money in those days) he would enthuse as he fingered my new Harris Tweed jacket. At that time, a major career success would be to earn £1,000 a year – which was incidentally the income Mr Jeavons our physics master claimed to earn, when he added private tutoring to his salary.

Sloane Grammar made its overriding contribution to my life by giving me a good all-round education and, besides preparing me for university to become an aeronautical engineer (what else?), made me its school vice-captain.

As with most 16-year-olds, politics other than related to the war was of no great interest or consequence to me. But the 1942 Beverage Report proposing a Welfare State got my attention. By the population at large, it was taken as a breakthrough in care and fairness for everybody. However, with the benefit of hindsight, the opinion I offered my schoolmates, 'A Welfare State would sap the moral fibre of the nation', could well be considered wisdom: 'out of the mouths of babes and sucklings …'

On VE Day, I was one of several hundred thousands who surged in Whitehall outside the Ministry of Health building shouting in unison, 'We want Winnie', until Churchill came out on the big balcony with his Cabinet, to wave in victory.

29 August 1946 – also from Huddersfield

Dear Mum, Dad & Andrew,

Thanks very much for your letter which I received on Monday. I'm, afraid our letters crossed. I am really happy that Dad's X ray was favourable, & let us hope that the whole trouble is clearing up.

Fancy giving Jimmy Jnr. away after all, I thought we were going to keep him now. I hope Jimmy[38] is running like a Delage now. By the way Andrew, your memory is like a sieve. The petrol bloke's name is Shell and he lives in Kings road near Parson's Green, on a corner on the Parson's Green side there is a baker's shop; remember?

About the fountain pen, Mr. Dixon[39] ought to have it, as I gave him it to him on the last day of camp. The badges, as you know, I have not been able to get yet.

I have written to Mr. Dixon, and told him when I am coming home. It is a pity, I can't be at the Scouters[40] meeting on Friday, but it can't be helped. I had a letter from John & he says he will be there. Andrew could you tell him that I shall call round on Sunday C. of H.[41] I have also heard from Pat Talfourd.[42]

Poor Mother, having to be in all day again. The sooner it is over the better.

I shall be leaving Huddersfield by the 8.38 train, and will arrive at Euston at 2.25 p.m. So if anybody can meet me, I would very much appreciate it.

Yesterday we went to Barnsley which is not far from here, in hope of finding Tony Randall, but at the Hostel, the receptionist girl said, 'Randall? Oh from Canvey Island, he's been away for months' [he was a Bevin Boy[43] and ran away, to join the Fleet Air Arm]. Then we had a high tea which cost us 4/- each. I am fair broke now.

It is pouring with rain now, and when I have finished this letter, we are going to have a look at a museum.

Last night we had a look at a local Scout troop, and to-morrow we shall see the local cubs. On the whole I have had a really enjoyable time, so you need not worry. If I come home with a Yorkshire accent, don't be surprised.

I must close now, so cheerio for now & love to all from your John

Andrew and John, around 1944. (Author's collection)

Epilogue

Andrew qualified as a doctor in 1947 and became a consultant anaesthetist. I (perhaps after following Andrew's good advice) matriculated with four Distinctions and three Credits in 1945 (Andrew had received three Distinctions and four Credits!) and after Higher Schools/Inter BSc in 1947. With floods of servicemen returning from the war I was unable to get onto a full-time degree course, instead attending London's Northampton Polytechnic for Aeronautical Engineering two days a week. I qualified in 1950 with a University of London B.Sc. (engineering) degree, having completed the degree in the same time as the full-time students.

On reaching the age of 21, we respectively became British Subjects by Naturalisation. Andrew served two years of National Service as a medical officer in the army; his successful medical career in London eventually led to his immigration to the USA, where he continued practising anaesthesia and much work with the Christian Church.

After spending time as a Missionary in India, Andrew married at the relatively advanced age of 34, to a dietician and fellow missionary in India. They had two sons and his family also immigrated to the USA, where Andrew and his wife gained four grandchildren.

I became an aeronautical engineer, working on highly secret guided weapons at Vickers-Armstrongs (Aircraft) Ltd. While at Vickers, I learned to fly powered planes and gained my private pilot's license. I remained in defence-related positions until I became the entrepreneurial managing director of an engineering company, where I built a dominantly export-led business in automobile safety and in security systems – financed by 'bootstrapping'.

I married at the age of 24 to an opera singer; we had five children and ten grandchildren. At the age of 52 I lost everything to unethical 'partners' and, with nothing, immigrated to the USA where I started my own businesses and remained until retiring at age 73. Having realised my 'American dream', I retired with savings and the proceeds from selling my company.

Without doubt, our evacuation experiences involving hardship, poverty and loneliness away from our parents and family contributed to both our resilience and our subsequent determination to overcome difficulties. It helped us to make a success of our careers – and of our life-long marriages. We remained very busy into our 80s.

Afterword

By Andrew Forbat

It is interesting to look back on these letters after the passage of over seventy years. Even if some of the details have become dim with time, the experience is still very real to me. We had come from Hungary only three years before the outbreak of the war. Our parents still had the ideas of a middle-class, non-practicing Jewish family. Evacuation gave us our first experience of living with a gentile English family and the different standards and attitudes to be expected. Our English was adequate, but not nearly perfect, either in accent or vocabulary. I notice in reading these letters, that when Mr Kelly scolded me I wrote he kept interrogating me – when I meant interrupting! Afterwards, we were immersed in the English language, so that the entire experience was very educational.

Communication with our parents had to be by mail. A telephone call from Melksham would have necessitated a trunk call and we could not use our hosts' phone for that. On the other hand, in England, we could rely on a letter mailed before the last collection to arrive at its destination by the following morning.

We did not realise at the time the great danger in which Britain was. There was never any doubt in our minds that the Allies would have victory and that Hitler would be defeated. Despite shortages, rationing, blackout and hardships, there has never been a greater sense of unity and co-operation among the British people. We had a united purpose and determination, and it is our privilege to have experienced those days.

Notes

1   3*d* is 3 (old) pennies. Half a crown was worth 2/6.
2   Our grandfather was visiting from Hungary.
3   Granny, who we also called Noni, was Hungarian.
4   Mariska was our Hungarian maid.
5   Fasting for Yom Kippur.
6   Mr Young was our Scoutmaster in Fulham.
7   Tiggy was the cat.
8   Our lodger, at that time, a young Czech.
9   A Hungarian pastry delicacy.
10 A pastry delicacy that translates as 'Feminine Spirit'.
11 Raymond Newnham was a friend from the restaurant in the base-
    ment of my parents' house.
12 A small *Beigli* was a loaf.
13 A schoolmaster.
14 The local lorry firm driver.
15 A First World War soldiers' song.
16 A billeting officer.
17 Zsuzsi was our cousin in Budapest.
18 Uncle Arthur was sent to America, aged 18, in 1911.
19 Manager at W.H. Smith.
20 Uncle Eugene's milk bar.
21 Slang for shilling.

22 Dad was expecting a job in Evesham with the BBC listening to German broadcasts and translating intelligence.

23 'Oscar' was Andrew's nickname, given by the Scouts.

24 John's familiarity with Mr Redfearn's actual nickname.

25 A Scoutmaster.

26 Dr Cavell's nickname.

27 Tom was an ex-Scout, an RAF serviceman stationed in Melksham in 1941.

28 Aunt Edith.

29 Andrew's real question was: is he also to be interned? He never was.

30 Uncle Imre, also interned on the Isle of Man.

31 Francis Áldor, a friend of Dad's from Hungary.

32 Under-training as a toolmaker – to which Dad was totally unsuited.

33 Sheila Christian, Andrew's girlfriend.

34 Hungarian apple pie.

35 *Puszi* are kisses.

36 With school friend Alex Fullick, staying with his auntie.

37 French Rover Scout befriended at summer camp.

38 The new Morris 8 car.

39 The current Scoutmaster.

40 Scout leaders' meeting.

41 Court of Honour (a regular council of Scouts).

42 A female Cubmaster.

43 Compulsory war service initiated by Ernest Bevin, Minister of Labour.